Praise to God

by

Kathleen Higham

Printed and bound in the United States of America

ISBN **978-0-9896973-1-6**

First printing 2015

Words of Life Publishing

Books Written by Kathleen Higham

So Close to God
The Window to God
Two Faces
Reflections from God
Hidden in Christ with God

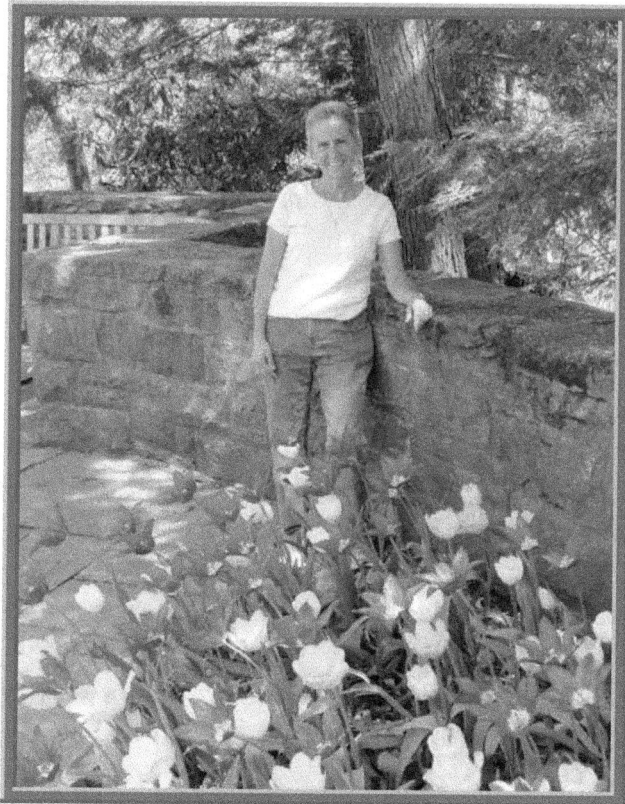

Photo Credit: Jim Higham

Author Kathleen Higham, on a beautiful
Spring day enjoying Mill Creek Park.

Acknowledgements

First and always, I thank my Savior, Jesus Christ. His living words endure forever. He is the true inspiration behind everything I write!

To my editor and dear friend, Gloria Dingeldein, who makes every book possible, I cannot thank you enough. Gloria is a professional with the patience of Job! She is my spiritual advisor, my dear friend and a very gifted woman of God. Once again, I must say there would be no book without God's divine inspiration and Gloria's touch.

A very heartfelt and special thank you to Kathleen Denis for her exquisite art work that she so kindly allows me to display on the covers of all my books.

I want to express my gratitude to my newest friend and brilliant graphic designer, Beth Basista. I thank you for the stunning book cover that you so expertly create and finalize with your excellent touch. She wraps her beautiful talent around God's words with complete elegance.

I also wish to thank my dear friend and amazing prayer warrior, Brenda Sereday, for writing the Foreword. She is a humble servant, speaker for *Stonecroft Ministry*, a Grief Minister of Sheepfold Ministry, Board Member of *Jesus Save America*, and a devoted member of *Victory Christian Center* for over 21 years.

Lastly, I wish to thank Diane Zawilinsky, for writing a few words about me. She is my long-time confidant, spiritual advisor, prayer partner and precious friend.

I also want to lovingly acknowledge some of the most wonderful dear ones, who have recently gone on to heaven: James Higham, Wendy Goldberg, Chloe Cox, Mrs. Imogene Canby, Major General George Smith, Debbie Craig, and Danielle Samarco.

In Christ,

Kathleen Higham

Foreword

Praise to God . . .

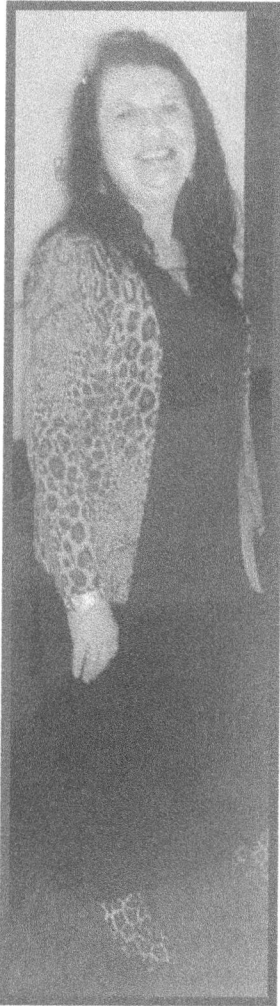

To be an exceptional writer, I believe it takes two things. To be a good listener, and a doer. Kathleen Higham is both. She listens intently to God, and then she faithfully writes it down by hand into one of her notebooks. Those God-inspired writings and eloquent, yet profound poetic expressions, have encouraged and inspired many. I have been one of those recipients who have been privileged to benefit from the gifts God has given her. She is a true poet and word smith that ministers to the soul, using everyday experiences and situations as her canvas, she interweaves descriptions of fierce storms, magnificent humming birds, gorgeous flowers, fantastic friendships, the beauty of life and the hope of everlasting life after death. She paints pictures with well chosen words that clearly reveal the love our Savior Jesus Christ has so dearly bestowed upon mankind. She shares deeply from her experience with grief and loss, but through her veil of tears, she points us to the cross and to our heavenly home. Her dependence on the word of God to meet every circumstance of life, echoes through every poem and story. I encourage you to keep this book close, because I have found that Kathleen's inspired words minister to me time and time again.

A beautiful scripture that reflects Kathleen's heart and writings declares: ***Praise the LORD, my soul; all my inmost being, praise His holy name.*** Psalm 103:1 (NIV). I believe that is what Kathleen does with the poetry and stories written in this book as she gives us hope that one day, we will be praising God together with those who have gone on to glory before us. May you be richly blessed.

Brenda D. Sereday

Dedication

I dedicate this book to James Paul Higham, my beautiful husband and best friend. Jim was a godly man and I miss his wisdom and gentle ways. He went home to be with the Lord on September 16, 2013. Until we meet again I love you now and forever.

As Always,

Kathleen Higham

James Paul Higham

When I think of kindness
I think of Jim
Selfless helpful acts
Wherever he's been

Like a brother
To many a friend
Acts of kindness
A natural for Jim

Inspiration for living
Giving encouragement
Each and every day
In his special way

A kind and gentle spirit
Thoughtful, caring too
Finding words to comfort
Love to carry you

Precious memories
Will still live on
His love always
Lingers on and on

Now in Heaven
Now at peace
Celebrating Jesus
Till again we meet

❧

Jim was an avid runner and athlete. He ran a total of 22 marathons, which included the Boston Marathon. He was a godly man who followed a simple philosophy, "If something bothers you, just don't think about it."

His Song

Softly in the twilight of the hour
I hear His voice and tremble with His power
The heavens breathe a holy lullaby
My slumber interrupts me with a sigh

In the night I hear Him sing a prayer
A rhapsody so tender fills the air
The silent tear may fall before I cry
But, peace will come and claim me if I die

Sleeping sweetly, sweetly by my side
His song of love can never be denied
The sound flows oh so gently to my ear
My Father comes and sings away my fear

How I long to see His face in glory
Touch the lips that tell the lovers story
Lovingly He comes and draws me near
When His music calls my name, He's here

There is no time to ponder life this day
His symphony has wildly come to play
Unimaginable joy walked through my door
Before I wake my soul cries out for more

Take my hand I love you so my child
Your heart must be completely reconciled
This melody redeems, redeems your soul
I will sing a song to make you whole

How I long to see His face in glory
Touch the lips that tell the lovers story
Lovingly He comes and draws me near
When the music calls my name, He's here

Never will I leave for you are mine
When you're dreaming you will see a sign
Before the morning faces with the dawn
My song will linger, linger, linger on

Open up your eyes and feel my kiss
You were born for such a time as this
The sun will shine and warm you all day long
Come to me my child and sing my song

How I long to see His face in glory
Touch the lips that tell the lovers story
Lovingly He comes and draws me near
When the music calls my name, He's here

Sleeping sweetly, sweetly by my side
His song of love can never be denied
The sound flows oh so gently to my ear
My Father comes and sings away my fear

❧❧

The LORD will command His lovingkindness in the daytime,
And in the night His song shall be with me-
A prayer to the God of my life.
Psalm 42:8 (NKJV)

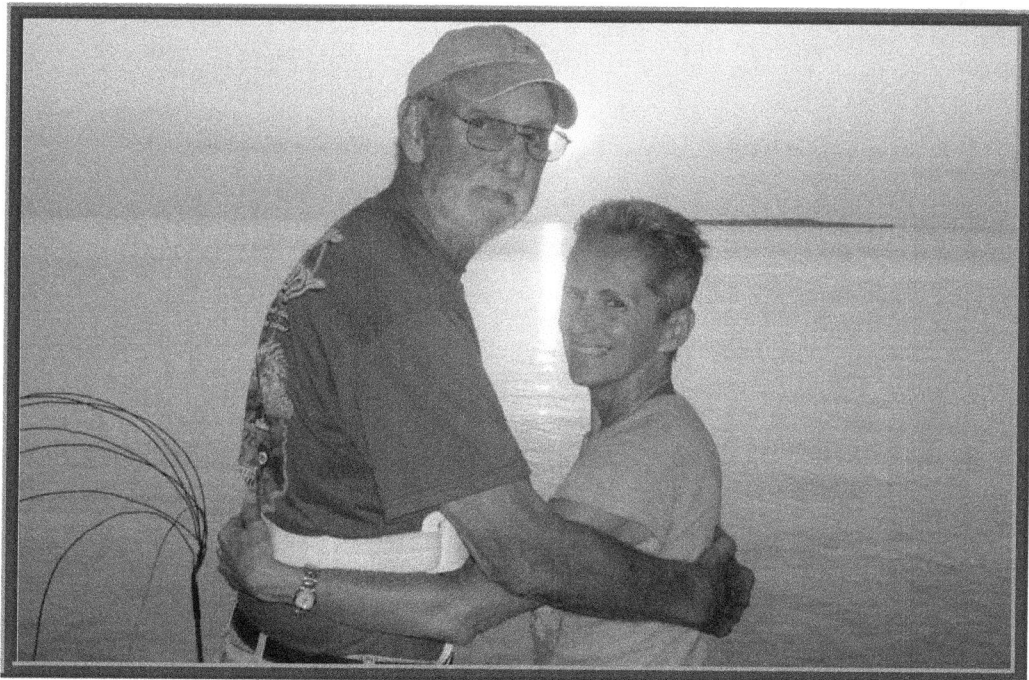

Table of Contents

A Flower's Bloom

If a flower's bloom could see, would she look to the heavens in search of Thee?

If a flower's bloom could hear, would she open up her petals as His footsteps draw near?

If a flower's bloom could speak, would she say, "Lord, crush me first so I may sweetly reek?"

If a flower's bloom could cry, would she lift her petals glistening with tears to the sky?

If a flower's bloom could pray, would she say, "Take me from these acres where I lay?"

If a flower's bloom could sing, would she pour out her essence unto every living thing?

If a flower's bloom could teach, would she stretch out her beauty to all that she could reach?

If a flower's bloom could fly, would she leap into the arms of God the Father on High?

If a flower's bloom could run, would she make haste to blossom and meet the Son?

If a flower's bloom could need, would she revel in the planting of the seed?

If a flower's bloom could grieve, would she close shut her petals tight and leave?

If a flower's bloom could fall, would she long to be trampled under the foot of Your call?

If a flower's bloom could know, would she choose another place to go?

If a flower's bloom could feel, would she release the nectar of her balm to heal?

If a flower's bloom could do, would she acknowledge that she was picked by You?

If a flower's bloom could live, would she find another way to give?

If a flower's bloom could sigh, would she understand that God created her to die?

If a flower's bloom could choose, would she surrender her life to God and gladly lose?

If a flower's bloom could be, would she share her most alluring scent with me?

If we could be as a flower's bloom, would we cast aside this life of gloom and doom?

If we could grasp the vastness of the flowers in full bloom;

Flowers crushed and bent for just one drop of her sweet perfume.

If we could know at last the enormity of the flower's worth;

For we are born, instilled with this scent of life at our birth.

Therefore, no evilness or sorrow would dare to loom,

Over this lovely gift from God---A flower's bloom...

An Angel Sings Story

How I love to write of angelic things. Now a tender moment carries me to fluttering wings. It is a windy, dark and dreary morn. The trees begin to bend and sway. Branches are slapping wildly in the wind. No critters venture out to seize the day. This is a perfect time to ponder life and the critters hiding wisely in the maze of woods behind our house. I see nary a bird, a lizard, or even a bug. It seems these creatures of God remain safe and snug. I shall remain as well, protected in my house from the storm that threatens to come. Oh, it surely is a windy, dark, and dreary morn. Yet, much to my delight, I witness an incredible sight. A hummingbird so tiny zips by with wings fluttering rapidly in flight. She flies into the storm in search of sustenance. We have always provided the sweet nectar for our precious guest. Now the most delicate of creatures perches upon the feeder to partake and rest.

A miracle of peace forbears the scene. This miniature creature does not preen. Awe comes when the winds surrounds and pounds her little chest. Still, she holds firm in her quest. She is not bothered by the raging wind that keeps others hiding from this display of power that sounds like an angry beast. No! For this tiny one has come in faith and trust to feast. I am incredulous of the strength within this most delicate bird. She flits away as if nothing unusual has occurred. The rain falls in blinding sheets, almost completely obscures my view, but I strain my eyes to see. She comes against the fiercest wind and rain, appearing oblivious to any pain. She comes for sustenance and shares His peace.

Now here I sit and contemplate the vision as the world has gone mad and insanity rules, it seems. But, for a God who protects and guards our hearts and all our dreams; for we are not small, nor insignificant. Do not hide away from the looming storms of life that will attack. Fly; fly into the storm fearing naught. He goes before you and prepares the way. Sustenance is waiting in the fierceness of the winds that blow. Fly, fly into the storm and you will know. Be as the hummingbird with strength so bold. Even when the tiniest wings unfold; convinced that no power, no wind, no storms of life will keep His Word untold. Fly into the storm and soar. Drink the sustenance He gives and far, far more. Observe the power of the vision of this creature He designed to be so small.

As rain pours down, wind blows mightily against her breast, yet she chirps to Him a "thank you." It was a barely audible sound and I wondered if I truly heard her precious call. Yes, God allowed me to hear the sound of joy and feel His everlasting peace that He longs to give to one and all. The lesson is to know the battle is won. The strength and power is not of massive wealth or size. The strength comes when seen through our own eyes that even the smallest, He will use to teach.

The storms may battle, but our souls are out of reach. If like the hummingbird, you have one goal. Then listen to the sound of fragile wings, and hear the sweetest chirp, when from her heart an angel sings…

An Angel Sings

Oh, what a dark and dreary day
My pencil has very little to say
But how the poet longs to write
As I see this most amazing sight.

Rain fiercely pours down outside
Yet to the feeder she will glide
A hummingbird so incredibly small
I could scarcely see her at all.

Wind and rain beat upon her breast
Still she perched sweetly in her quest
Not deterred by the fearsome storm
That brutalized her delicate form.

I stared in awe at this little one
Who needed not the warming sun
Feasting from a feeder majestically
Then a whisper of sound, unbelievably.

Almost inaudible the chirp, I heard
"Thank you Lord," from the fragile bird
Oh, praise God for her fluttering wings
When from her heart an angel sings…

Painting by Kathleen Denis © *The Hummingbird Garden.*

ℰ℅℈

*Sustain me, my God, according to your promise,
and I will live; do not let my hopes be dashed.*
Psalm 119:116 (NIV)

3

A Job Moment Story

I often discuss with my friend, Stephanie, the oppressiveness of human suffering. Lately it seems so many are in the thick of it. Those who have been overwhelmingly attacked, have stood in the fiery furnace of imminent meltdown, but they waited on God to protect them. We surely cannot know why some feel the punch, the brutality of life and others just a stinging slap; but it is not in the blow or sting that reveals the strength of He who is in you. The reflection comes almost in a blinding glare from those who are completely trusting God in these times that are undeniably unfair. It is "A Job Moment."

The suffering of Job, though incomprehensible, was of short duration, and after the trial, he was blessed even more than one could imagine. Oh it surely was a vicious punch, but the sting of life became the unimaginable joy of life after the pain.

Well, I have heard this saying as a runner, "No pain, no gain." Did that surface in a roundabout way from Job? "No pain, no gain." Maybe, but I believe that one's pain is uniquely ours in that it can be vastly different and seemingly unfair to the human mind, yet, pain is pain regardless of the route it travels. Pain is pain.

I was reminded of this as I snapped one shot after another of a bumblebee dancing from flower to flower in my backyard. To me this creature was breathtakingly beautiful. It was one of those moments in life when time stands still and we can feel joy in God's creativity. The flower dance, as I call it, held me spell bound for some time, until that bee buzzed me and chased me, and then, it quickly turned to hell bound! The bumblebee, the flowers, and the sweetness of all that surrounds us can keep us in the moment, until the attack! You see dear friends, the incredible winged creature has a stinger and though it looks docile, this tiny one can cause enormous pain.

The lesson: I doubt any of us will escape some form of pain in our lifetime. Whatever our walk in life no matter how beautiful it appears to others, pain flits about. Most assuredly, we will feel the sting of life, and even possibly, the knockout punch might become your "Job Moment."

I remember years ago these taunting words of a well-known boxer, Muhammad Ali, "Float like a butterfly, sting like a bee." But here is the good news; whatever or however your "Job Moment" is delivered, we know it is only temporary! God has something in store for us that we cannot know.

Praise Him for this one absolute in life; there will be gain, there will be pain, but at the end of this life there will be far more, waiting, waiting behind Heaven's door. Pain and gain is the double-edged sword, and your life is held firmly, by the Hand of our Lord…

4

A Job Moment

Our prayers are avalanching
The list of suffering will bear
Name after name of loved ones
This life does not speak fair.

Yet, none can understand this
And the pain is always there
A punch, a sting, who knows, but
Most assuredly we all will share.

The sting of life not really unfair
For the pain of Christ we abhor
But the doors of heaven are waiting
Our Savior longs to give us more.

No pain, no gain, no matter
When a Job Moment will come
The scales may be unjustly balanced
And more fair to a certain some.

Remember to trust in the Father God
Who commands the double-edged
sword
As a Job Moment is your salvation
Held secure by the Hand of our Lord.

❧

They surrounded me like bees;
They quenched like a fire of thorns;
For in the name of the Lord I will destroy them.
You pushed me violently, that I might fall,
But the LORD helped me.
The LORD is my strength and song,
And has become my salvation.
Psalm 118:12-14 (NKJV)

5

Between Here And Heaven Story

Yesterday has been erased as it needed to be. Words not of God were spoken and a heart was debased. To claim another's pain will fill the devil with glee. So it has been erased, now move on and see. A text message 'pings' this very day. A young woman weeps for a husband who suddenly passed away. Another struck down, though much older, but still her life hangs in the balance as we pray. A circumstance in which the body fights in savage pain to live. This morning begins and heartache comes swiftly as if through a sieve. Claim this day to stop and praise our Lord. It's true there are some who have already gone, but for those of uncertainty, we must continue to pray. For uncertainty is more than just a word. However, not many recognize the enormity of this word until it becomes a reality. Some are waiting precariously in that place **between here and heaven**.

Uncertainty has always been here where we exist. From the moment of our birth uncertainty began and shall persist. Yet it might hide for decades until old age, but uncertainty will touch every last one of us as sure as I am writing about it on this page. So then, what shall we do besides the obvious answer, to pray? Can life be beautiful between here and heaven, or must it be a constant burden at best? There must be many moments of stunning joy, exhilarating and exquisite moments that offset the most difficult test. If one can live and walk with God through every second of life's quest; what can be learned from the quest? Learn from the past and make today be of value. Remember your youthful days.

When I was young, I planted trees in my front yard. I did not plan strategically where to plant them, or study what kind of tree to plant. Thirty-five years later, I have had to remove many of the trees because they have grown into power lines, their roots have broken drain tile, and they have cluttered my yard with useless seedlings. It took all these years to realize that unwise planning caused considerable damage. This week my husband asks me if I would like to plant a young sapling, a Crimson King Maple tree that our neighbor has offered to us. It surely will be a fabulous tree someday, but not thinking it through I said, "No, why bother? We will not live long enough to see it grow or enjoy its beauty." This morning as the message and phone calls come for prayer requests, there is a lesson from God who instructs, if my heart is open to hear. He says, "If you plant the tree now in a perfect place to grow, someday another will share the beauty of the tree." Well, the selfishness of my heart missed it. I simply did not see. I do not need to be the one who enjoys the tree. Twenty or thirty years from now, if this world should still exist, someone may gaze upon the tree and not have missed all that I have missed when I centered on myself, believing life was all about me. A decision was made, and if meant to be, I told my husband, "Go and get that tree." We are between here and heaven, but we are much closer to heaven than here. Though the decision comes with a sigh---I pray for peace and cast aside the heaviness of fear, because of the goodness that has been given to me in the gift of this tiny tree. We must live our last days with a little leaven; for we are closer than ever to **between here and heaven...**

Between Here And Heaven

A song recently sung
Memories when I was young
Time flew furious, fast
Life here, not to last.

Here today, gone tomorrow
A cliché many borrow
Heaven, a breath away
Might be even today.

There is much to be done
Just meet the rising sun
Then look back in shock
Of life, take stock.

Uncertainty comes to claim
Having no rise to fame
Uncertainty lies between
Every human being.

Youth may live here
But age draws near
Heaven about to touch
So give, give much.

Leave behind and do
Share a remembrance of you
All selfishness put away
Plant a tree today.

Let go of the past
Then heavy fear, cast
Live with a little leaven
Between here and heaven.

❧

. . . you do not know what will happen tomorrow. For what is your life? It is even a vapor that appears for a little time and then vanishes away. James 4:14 (NKJV)

Burning Hearts Story

Once again God gave me another sunset story. In the Summer of 2013, I met a lovely woman from Michigan while in the Keys. She was invited by the property owner to watch the sunset. It was an extraordinary skyline, but we were the only two willing to brave the cold and vicious winds to watch the sunset.

The sea was rough and waves crashed against the break wall. The winds blew a blunted moaning sound accompanied by a burst of icy stinging mist that took our breath away, but when the moment came we both cried out in unison, "Look the sun is shaped like a heart!" It held me in a paralytic state until I finally put my camera to the sky and snapped the picture.

Oh, but it was not meant to be, and this most mesmerizing sunset was not captured on film. I admit there was disappointment at having missed this astonishing image that surely was a gift from God! Twice this month I was unable to capture the exquisite and unbelievable creativity of my Father God. Now I am speaking of it in awe because there were two of us to witness and agree that the incredible sight did indeed happen.

I was not able to visually record the sight which would have been a major accomplishment. In retrospect, the moment shared with my new friend, Heidi, occurred so that we in turn, could share what I felt was the depiction of the burning heart of God. It was fleeting, but stunning, as it silently vanished into the horizon.

Could it be that our Lord gave us a peek into history? Maybe it was a much needed reminder of the Son, His Son, who gave His heart for us on a wooden cross. There were no pictures then, but those that witnessed it told the story, and thousands upon thousands believed.

Now I share this story and I expect my friend will share the story of the night we stood shoulder to shoulder, as sisters in the Kingdom of God, and briefly experienced a very Holy sight. We saw the heart of God, then watched it slip slowly into the fading light. These are treasured moments that God shares for His reasons. All we have to do is open our hearts and be one with Him. If we will surrender, there will be countless moments that will inspire and bring peace and hope to the heart that longs. Just wait and trust in Him, for the God moments to come unexpectedly and joyfully.

Look to the sky
Look to the ground
Look to the tree
And finally, look to the sea
As the burning heart of God
Gives witness to you and me.

Burning Hearts

Photo credit: Kent Viklund

Was it the burning heart of God?
As the sun set in glory and awe
Was it the burning heart of God?
My eyes questioned what I saw.

It was absolutely incredible
Though the moment was very brief
A warmth poured over my soul
Then authenticated my belief.

My belief in the Father God
Who sent to us His only Son
Now my eyes have witnessed this
The heart shaped setting sun.

A God moment of all times
His holiness sweeps through me
Was it the burning heart of God?
That I was privileged to see?

Now my heart burns for His
And the sight I will never forget
The night I saw His burning heart
Shared with a new friend, another sunset…

ৎৎঌ

"Did not our hearts burn within us
while He talked with us on the road,
and while he opened the Scriptures to us?"
Luke 24:32 (NKJV)

9

But For Now Story

There is no place that cannot be touched by His spiritual embrace. I find myself reading my own devotionals more and more. The shocking revelation comes to me that God wrote the book to minister to not only those in need, but especially to the hand that held the pencil.

Some things never change. I was forced to use a computer when I began to write prolifically, but after all these years I still hand write with my pencil, every single word God gives to me. God continues to bless me with wonderful tidbits from His heart to mine. There are times when I feel the darkness closing in and because I know my Father God is light, I do not fear being in this particular place, for there is no place that cannot be touched by His spiritual embrace. It is impossible to be alone when you have committed your life to God.

It may seem as though I am by myself as I wait for news from the doctor about my Jim, but the truth is: I am never alone! It has been a common occurrence these past five years that I find myself waiting for the doctor as Jim is getting a surgery or heart procedure.

My daughter and I have the same text message every time Jim is admitted to the cardiac unit.

She texts me: "Are you alone?"

Of course she knows that I am always alone in the aspect that there is no person sitting with me as I wait. I text her: "No, I am not alone; God is here." ☺

She texts me back: "You know what I mean Mother." ☹

When my daughter calls me Mother it is her way of telling me that she is serious! The thing is I was never more serious in my life! I am not alone. Even when enticed by fear of the unknown, I wait quietly, for I am never alone. I am surrendered to the belief that someday I shall see His face. But for now I feel Him. But for now I am touched by His spiritual embrace…

∽✥∾

And the LORD, he it is that doth go before thee;
he will be with thee, he will not fail thee, neither forsake thee:
fear not, neither be dismayed.
Deuteronomy 31:8 (KJV)

But For Now

Here I sit quietly and wait
Praise God, then contemplate
I've been here many times before
My eyes drift often to the door.

Yet, here I sit quietly and wait
There is no anxiety for our fate
God comforts me in this place
Touched by His spiritual embrace.

Here I sit quietly and wait
The hour comes not a moment late
My prayer now an audible moan
For I am never ever alone.

But for now, I feel His touch
Oh God loves me so very much
Someday I shall see His face
But for now, feel His spiritual embrace.

෯෴

Have you not known? Have you not heard?
The everlasting God, the LORD,
The Creator of the ends of the earth,
Neither faints nor is weary.
His understanding is unsearchable.
He gives power to the weak, And to those who have no might
He increases strength. Even the youths shall faint and be weary,
And the young men shall utterly fall,
But those who wait on the LORD
Shall renew their strength;
They shall mount up with wings like eagles,
They shall run and not be weary,
They shall walk and not faint.
Isaiah 40: 28-31 (NKJV)

Come Sit With Me Awhile

Come and sit with me awhile
Why could I not be still?
Just a sweet, tender request
Sometimes I failed to fulfil.

Come and sit with me awhile
For I may not always be here
Needing a little time from you
Time we will both hold dear.

Come and sit with me awhile
Before my time is gone
When tears will bring you to me
In the hours before the dawn.

Come and sit with me awhile
We don't even have to talk
Just come, just come, my child
We'll take a quiet walk.

Come and sit with me awhile
So quickly comes tomorrow
I pray for your presence
A moment I might borrow.

Come and sit with me awhile
Only one can love you more
My God, your God, our God
He waits at Heaven's door.

Come and sit with me awhile
For with Him I will leave
It may be unexpectedly
Your heart will not conceive.

Come and sit with me awhile
Remembering my Mother's voice
Come and sit with me awhile
Someday, there will be no choice.

Come and sit with me awhile
Warm eyes will tenderly greet
A Mother's heart will touch you
When together we shall meet.

Come and sit with me awhile
I can feel my Mother's smile
She waits patiently in Heaven saying,
"Come and sit with me awhile."

Control Story

One must be out of control to be in control. Sometimes things interrupt our lives and press down hard the fact that we have absolutely no control over life in certain circumstances. We have no control at all! It can become a terrifying place to be when this revelation washes over you. The hardest part of knowing that you cannot control a given situation is understanding and believing who is in control. It is easy to praise God and acknowledge His greatness, power, majesty, and yes we often say, "God is in control." But, when that moment of terror comes and there is a cold shaking experience that is unexplainable unless you are the one in the experience; everything is out of control and you feel numb, shocked, and helpless. You say the words, "He is in control." Then suddenly you wonder if He really is. I have heard someone say that God is not really in control and that is why the world is as it is—to say that God is not in control is scarier than knowing that I am not in control, because when everything is falling apart as it often will in this life, there must be a place of peace and comfort. God says, "My grace is sufficient." Are grace and control relative to each other? *For by grace are ye saved through faith; and that not of yourselves: it is the gift of God: not of works that any man should boast.* Ephesians 2:8-9 (KJV). So grace is God's favour on those who don't deserve it. *And we know that in all things God works for the good of those who love him, who have been called according to His purpose.* Romans 8:28 (NIV). *For I know the plans I have for you, declares the Lord, plans to prosper you and not to harm you, plans to give you hope and a future.* Jeremiah 29:11 (NIV). *God is not the author of confusion but of peace, as in all the churches of the saints.* I Corinthians 14:33 (NKJV) Our God is rich in mercy and grace and He chose to save us. Philippians 4:6-7 says to bring our petitions to the Lord, and so I shall do just that. *He was wounded for our transgressions, He was bruised for our iniquities; The chastisement for our peace was upon Him. And by His stripes we are healed.* Isaiah 53:5 (NKJV) His grace is sufficient, and He is in control…when I am surrendered to Him.

Control

Here, here, here
Take this cup from me
Fear, fear, fear
It is my fervent plea.

Pray, pray, pray
A heart cries to You
Help. Help. Help
Lord, help me through.

Praise, praise, praise
I must praise You first
Trust, trust, trust
Not one in Him is cursed.

Promised, promised, promised
So written in Your Word
Fled, fled, fled
Fear fled when I heard.

Draw The Line Story

Do you know where you are going? I know where I am going, because I know where God is. He is now here. There was a time when He was nowhere in my life. Well, actually He was somewhere near, hovering by my side. He was waiting for me to know that He was there. Ten years ago I finally felt Him there. God was no longer nowhere in my life, but He was now here.

You see, before I knew Him I wasn't conscious of the line between nowhere and now here—Once I moved forward just one letter and drew that line—There He was all that time! In a stroke He was now here. He has been here with me for a long time, and now that He is here, I am going there. Where? Well, I am going to Heaven. It is so incredible that one thin line changed my life forevermore. I am a citizen of Heaven! I am no longer going nowhere. At last I saw the sign and drew the line. Out of nowhere He came to claim, "You are mine!" Now might be the time to draw the line…

Draw The Line, God Is Now Here

When to draw the line?
Something I now know
God is here with me
And with Him I will go.

This was not always so
He hovered by my side
I was absolutely nowhere
My foolish heart denied.

One day I drew the line
Struggling all these years
I felt Him come to me
The line blurred my tears.

Oh, the glory of it all
For He is "now here"
No longer hovering near-by
My vision became so clear.

A life once going nowhere
Until I drew that line
He claimed me completely
Saying, "Child you are mine."

I'm a citizen of Heaven
With great faith I will share
The moment I drew the line
Well, God was waiting there.

It may be a fine line, but
His presence is so Divine
Nowhere, then "now here"'
Now; it's time to draw the line.

The LORD appeared to us in the past, saying: "I have loved you with an everlasting love; I have drawn you with unfailing kindness." **Jeremiah 31:3(NIV)**

Everything Story

On this dreary rainy morn, so often words from God are born. As I study, read and pray, I think of my loved ones who are struggling today. My devotional, ***Streams in the Desert*** speaks to me these simplistic encouraging words: "See God in everything, and God will calm and color all that thou dost see!." (***Streams in the Desert,*** September 17). Sometimes it is very hard to see God in everything when everything does not see God. There are so many who suffer and grieve, finding it difficult, at times to believe. The unknown has obstructed their intimate need to cleave. So even though God is everywhere and in everything, the preponderance of fear will silence the song that one might cry softly in the night. "Father God, I cannot sing one word for I am stunned with fright!" You are in everything; still I stumble in this fight. I cannot see everything in the oppressiveness of my plight.

Life. Life as I knew it left! I cannot even breathe; in agony I am bereft. Because fear has filled my very soul with dread as I lay wide-eyed on my bed. This body cannot lift its arms to pray; weighted down like lead. Yet deep inside there is hope. I remember my childhood days and the voice that echoes from the past, her praise. My mother sings and offers up her prayers, her pleas; even in times such as these---I can hear her song: "You are everything, my Lord. For You I shall always long." Tears come at last and drench the pillow for this memory of a mother's song. Now, now, I long; for it is so. No matter what the sorrow, I too shall sing---God, God is in everything!

Everything

Everything I thought I knew
From me in stunning shock, flew
Everything I thought I knew
Gone, gone, gone, it's true.

Now dazed, what shall it be?
My tears locked inside, not free
From these eyes that long to see
Lord, what will become of me?

Everything I thought I knew
Flees, flees! What can I do?
Everything I thought I knew
I cry, God let everything be You.

In this life of struggle, I thought
Even for those things I fought
But in this snare I am caught
Everything I thought I knew was not!

Hear the chimes, the bells will ring
And my voice finds You as I sing
A mother's song to You, I bring
God---God is in everything!
෨ඏ
You are my hiding place;
You shall preserve me from trouble;
You shall surround me with songs of
deliverance. **Psalm 32:7 (NKJV)**

Dealing Story

This morning, once again, a revelation comes from my favorite devotional, *My Utmost for His Highest*, by Oswald Chambers. It propels me to a deeper level with my Father God. The usual morning routine of prayer and study has been transformed by two sentences that stopped me for a moment to digress in my prayer request. There is a matter so preponderous that has preoccupied and superseded the most simplistic act of prayer. Health issues and fear can cause one's prayer life to alter, in that as we are crying out for help, we might unknowingly straddle the spiritual bond from Jesus Christ that hedges us in and protects us. Here is my friend Oswald's quote which draws me back to the very reason for prayer; "Quit praying about yourself and spend your life for the sake of others as the bond servant of Jesus," and then Oswald adds, "That is the true meaning of being broken bread and poured-out wine in real life." (*Utmost for His Highest*, Chambers, July 15, *My Life's Spiritual Honor and Duty*).

So the reality of what we are dealing with is not so much the fear of health issues, or the constant trials life can bring, but to me the biggest fear of all is that our faith will fail. Now the question is do we really trust God to heal us? I believe God is looking on from the heavens and there is nothing more for me to do, but trust in Him, believe, and pray.

Everyone has a private heartache that they are dealing with on a personal level. A lovely and precious woman shared her most intimate sorrow with me. No one is exempt from suffering. Even the grandest exterior may have a hidden crack within. Oh, we can cover, fix-up, and restore to near perfect, but in actuality there is no perfect life, but the one we will share with our Father God someday. So we will be dealing every day with our humanness. But, I praise God for this: He is healing!

Every moment that transpires is a process. We are dealing and He is healing! Life could not go on without this wonderful promise from Him. He will see us through. Do we hurt? Sometimes. Do we cry? Yes. Do we trust? We must! If you are hurting and not understanding what you are feeling, know this, while you are busy dealing, God is tenderly healing...

৵৽

The Spirit of the Lord GOD is upon me;
because the LORD hath anointed me to preach
good tidings unto the meek; he hath
sent me to bind up the brokenhearted,
to proclaim liberty to the captives, and the
opening of the prison to them that are bound;
Isaiah 61:1 (KJV)

Dealing

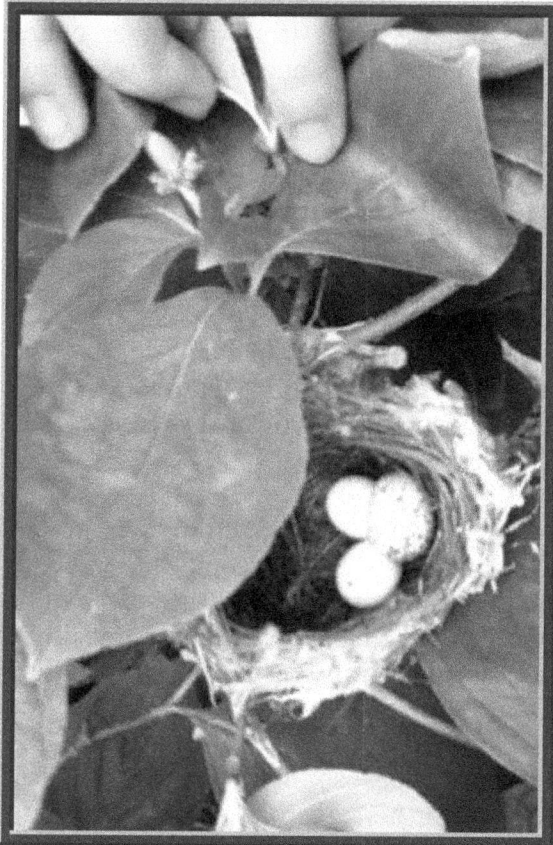

So, what are you dealing with?
We all know that life is unfair
And heartache will come to many
Yet through it, our God is there.

His heart will carry the burden
As He covets the soul you bare
Then asks you to pray for another
Life with Him means we must share.

So, what are you dealing with?
As you straddle the fence of fear?
Worry not, for God has hedged you in
Even if sometimes you cannot hear.

Now trust in Him, believe and pray
For in Christ only, we shall prevail
Broken and poured out as wine, but
Producing faith that will never fail.

So, what are you dealing with?
Are you struggling to feel real?
Know this: God in His infinite mercy
Reaches down from the heavens to heal...

✿✿

Have You not made a hedge around him,
around his household,
and around all that he has on every side?
You have blessed the work of his hands,
and his possessions have increased in the land.
Job 1:10 (NKJV)

17

Endless Sighs Story

In Loving Memory of James Paul Higham

Last week I received an email from a sweet young man that I sat beside on a flight to the Bahamas. He was on his way to an island mission's trip with other church members. We had a lovely chat and I would like to share this encouraging word from Daniel.

> Dear Kathleen, I am the police officer who sat beside you on the plane the other day. I just wanted to tell you it was a blessing to meet you. Two things that I really needed to hear was how to deal with my daughter and basketball and how you loved your husband. The way you talked about your husband and how good of a man he was made me look at the way I treat my wife and what would she say about me if I pass before her. I believe I treat my wife good, but I know I can be better which is my goal. I will always keep you and your family in prayer. Be blessed.

This morning I awake with a sigh. There has been much pondering and introspective searching for answers. It seems endless sighs have become the precedent that begins my day and ends the closing with the night that carries me to the solace of my bed. As a fragile human being I wonder what more could I have done to help my Jim? I wonder if he really knew of the powerful and extraordinary impact he had on my life as well as others. I wonder if he understood that I was completely overwhelmed by his love, compassion, goodness, and holiness.

Jim took me to places I may never have known because of who he was in Christ and how he loved. There was no pretence or motive for his generosity. He was capable of loving unconditionally and proved himself to be a gentleman of amazing tenderness. The only time I ever saw this man distressed or upset was if he thought someone purposefully hurt me.

Though I sigh over and over again, I know that someday the tears will dry, as the less I cry. Endless sighs will change to joyful cries. For I have moaned and groaned with agonizing loss only to reach the place that bears the Cross. Endless sighs may escape my lips for such a time as this; until the day I feel his kiss, soft and sweet.

Until the day I touch his face and stand with him on streets of gold; not to remember those times of old when his last breath and final tear paused as time stood still. My shattered heart wept for this---God's Will. Yet, understanding comforts me in knowing someday, we all will go home to God and hearts will soar—where endless sighs shall be no more...

Endless Sighs

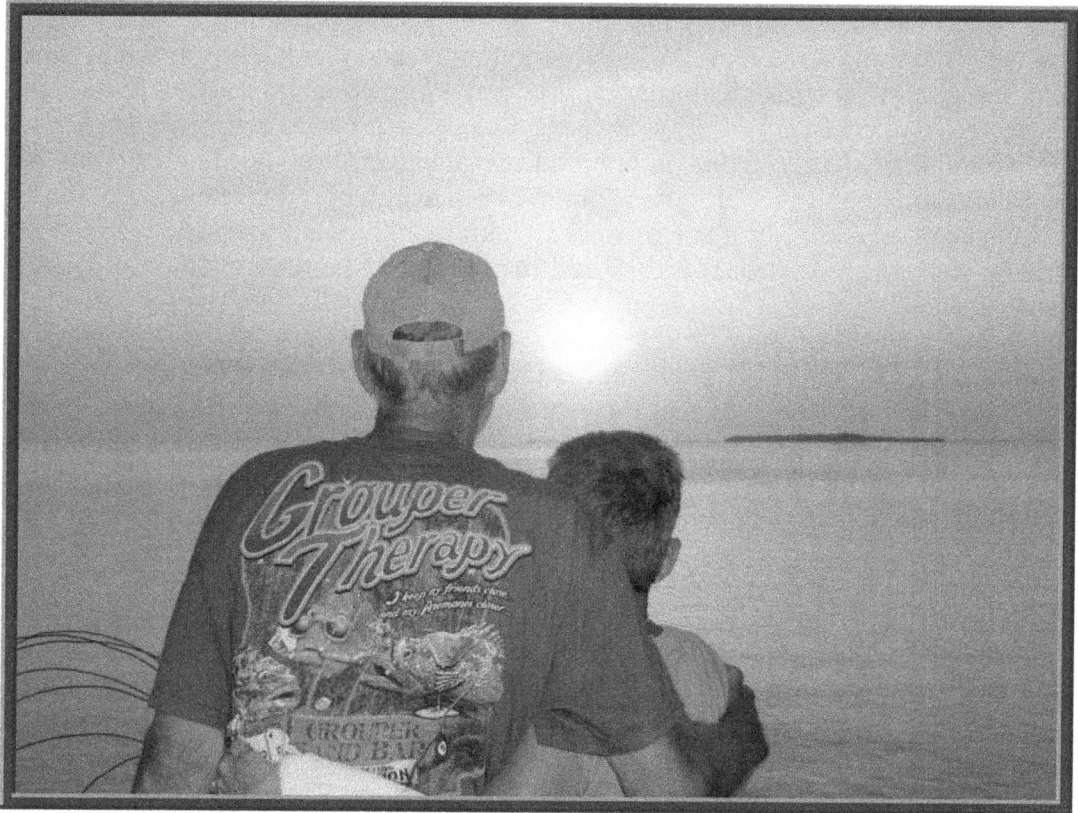

My eyes awaken to this cold and biting day
Longing for the sun, the clouds have kept at bay
God, my Father, comes to say, "You are not alone"
For if the sun should warm you constantly
You might not seek the solace of my love for thee
And if the clouds would drift open to the bluest skies
Denying the very reason for these times of endless sighs
You might not seek the tender mercies that I long to share
Then slip away not knowing how much I care
Yes, precious child of mine, it is a cold and biting day
Yet I am here to gather the falling tears, as you pray
Your soul calls to Me, see My light shines in sweet release
Loving fingers tenderly brush across your lips to cease
The Holy Spirit crushes your sorrow with His peace
Into the depth He flows deep to your soul's core
Alas, endless sighs be gone---Forevermore...

Even After The Sun Has Set Story

It is a cold, dark and rainy morning. Yesterday was a beautiful, warm and sunny day as we walked in Mill Creek Park. My thoughts raced inside my mind and time was running through me at a maddening pace. For just a few days ago a sweet friend had lost the race. She was only fifty-five years old. I can't help but wonder why such a lovely person would die so suddenly leaving behind two teenagers who needed her. She battled breast cancer and bone cancer for over four years. Then, without warning, she was struck down by a heart attack at her place of work. Unknowing, I went to see her. Her personal belongings sat on her desk. Her pillow still rested against her chair. But, my friend was no longer there.

There have been many tragic events this year, but this was the most sobering moment of disbelief, and grief would come later, along with the realization of the fragile state of one's immortality. For me, the profound disappointment comes not because my life is near completion, but for the devastated faces of those loved ones. I felt a wave of disappointment for the total ignorance of some who are so blessed by God, yet they take this life for granted, believing tomorrow always exists and they have earned the right to another day.

When one grows older, the gift comes in acknowledging, "the gift…" We have not earned one thing, nor are we promised the elusive tomorrow. If we wake up, so be it. He saw it fit. This morning, I reach for my notebook and my pencil in thankfulness. Should God allow me to finish this piece, or shall my pencil fall silently to the floor, to write no more? It is certainly a possibility, and brings a very important revelation as one ages.

We have no tomorrow; we have only this moment. If you stand before the sunset for another night, you must praise God for the blessed sight. But most of all, give to Him your heart and soul in the last hour before the night. If you have loved God with all your might, then give to Him the one hour before the inky black sky closes over you. This could be the very last sunset you shall ever see. Give thanks for your life before unbeknownst, it should flee.

Dear ones, there is time if you would recognize what God will do. For your loved ones, He glorified your name and left behind the sweetest memories of you. He is thoughtfully kind to leave behind; surely not a world of promises to come day after day. No! This life shall end and in the final hour; the earthly light shall fade away. What will you say? "Remember me." Oh precious one, remember Him, and what He lovingly designed. This is what our Lord would do. Even after the sun has set---your loved ones will remember you…

The Mighty One, God the LORD, Has spoken and called the earth
From the rising of the sun to its going down.
Psalm 50:1 (NKJV)

Even After The Sun Has Set

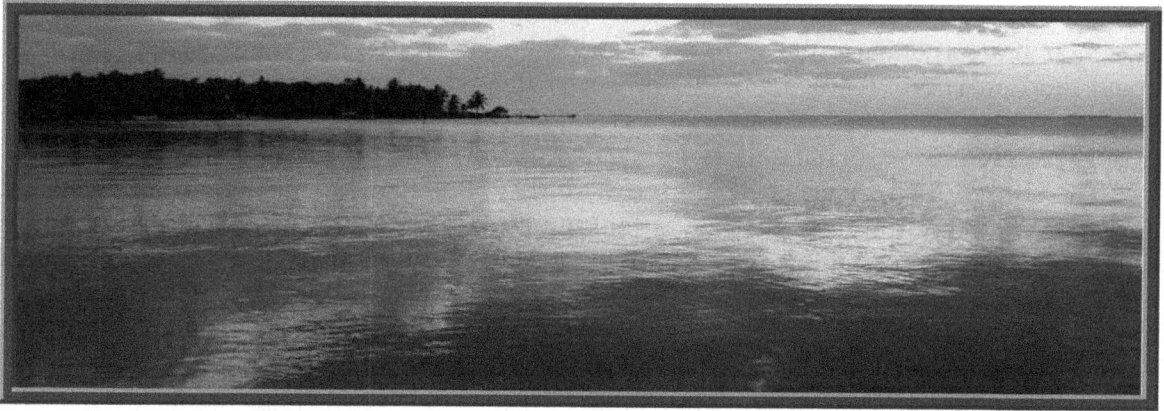

Even after the sun has set
Darkness does not claim the sky
It waits and hovers in wonder
For God to close it's eye.

There is much to do, dear ones
And there is even more to find
To Him, give your heart and soul
Then who you are, will be defined.

Now the hour of this beautiful day
For many will have just begun
But oh so quickly, it is gone
When to the West, sets the sun.

Thousands gone down in silence
On a dark-haired child of yesterday
From a babe in a mother's arms
To the one growing old and grey.

Yet there is time between the sunset
I believe, an hour, they say
Don't waste one precious moment
Fall to your knees and pray.

And if into an inky black sky
Your prayers seem to slip away
Do not worry, for God holds them
As He waits for the glorious day.

When the final sunset drifts slowly down
God remembers the hour of your birth
And from the darkness to the light
He will sweep you from this earth.

Oh glory comes from the Father
Unimaginable what He has designed
Because you gave your heart and soul
Sweet memories of you were left behind.

Even after the sun has set
There is nothing our Lord won't do
Even after the sun has set
Your loved ones will remember you…

❧ ❧

That they may know from the rising of the
sun to its setting That there is none besides
Me. I am the LORD, and there is no other;
Isaiah 45:6 (NKJV)

Eye To Eye Story

The first time I saw him, he was a little guy. Looking to his smiling face, we barely saw eye to eye. Oh, but how quickly the time has sped on by…

Is it a coincidence that a young man stands before the pulpit and speaks his heart about the Lord? No, it was God's plan. Truly this is an emotional time as I look to his smiling face again, and see the earnestness and sincerity of my teacher and my friend. He is only twenty-one years old and here I sit feeling very old, yet the man/boy is giving me a lesson so profound. I watched him grow in this church. He has hugged me time and again, but one day I noticed that I was looking up to eyes that sparkle and eyes that are wise. I felt the heart of this young man when he wrapped his arms around me. Here is a man of God, but only twenty-one, I think---young, young, young, but not a stumbling block! The sweetest story provided an understanding of all that has transpired this past week. A pastor and his wife, that are from the church Stephanie White grew up in, are visiting our church this Sunday. The visiting pastor's wife reveals to Stephanie that she remembers the day when Stephanie came to church shortly after the birth of her son. Stephanie carried the tiny bundle up to the front of the church and placed him on the altar, then prayed a mother's prayer. Oh my, here come the tears again as I hug my precious friend. You see, the boy who taught at the pulpit for the first time last Sunday, was Stephanie's son. And let me say this again, he is only twenty-one. Now I ask Stephanie this question, "How old were you when you placed your baby on that altar?" I saw her eyes widen in surprise as she whispered these words, "I was only twenty-one." Of course we had another moment here, but I must say that I do not believe it is the exactness in age of mother and son that touched me, but more the clarity that comes when we see eye to eye. I have always had the deepest respect for my friend as a writer and a teacher of God's Word. It is truly an honor to co-author devotionals with Stephanie White. Why? Well, she has been teaching me for over seven years now and I thought her to be young also, but she is old in God's Word. Last Sunday, when her child stood before us at the pulpit, I knew he was young, but more importantly, I knew that he was her son. I should not have been surprised when I looked into his eyes and saw that he was old in God's Word. *The eyes of those who see will not be dim,* Isaiah 32:3a (NKJV). ***Your watchmen shall lift up their voices, With their voices they shall sing together; For they shall see eye to eye When the Lord brings back Zion.*** Isaiah 52:8 (NKJV).

So, to see eye to eye, means to fully agree and be of the same opinion, and I am in agreement with this godly young man. I listened to him go deep and he made me weep. My tissue was soaked with tears as I wiped my eyes. It seems God gives us this window in time where we can look and see Him in those who have the gift. My heart searched and my soul reached out to seek the gift. I saw Eddie---eye to eye, just as I have seen his mother teach me over and over again. My eyes are filled with tears of joy for this young man who is my friend, as he comes full circle and stands in that very place where his mother has been. A tiny church trembles with the sweetest sigh---For a boy now a man that speaks God's Word---eye to eye…

Eye To Eye

I was mesmerized in my seat
Then stunned with surprise
Young, young, young, I thought
But he possessed old, old eyes.

What can this mean, I cry?
When the young now speak old?
"I want to know God for myself!"
He speaks these words so bold.

My tears poured down like rain
As I gazed upon his face
For he was tall as a mountain
His words would echo in this place.

"We have victory in our God!"
Step out and never forget!
Oh I remember this boy, a child
And the exact moment we met.

Now he teaches me as a man
From my lips a tender sigh
For his mother taught me first
How the years have sped on by.

A babe laid on the altar for God
His tiny eyes looking up
A mother prays for her son
Not knowing he would take the cup.

Amazing words this boy would speak
"We have enough faith to cause a riot!"
My soul leaped in the victory
He will not be tempered or quiet!

"I want to know God for myself!"
Well, so do I, so do I, I cry!
He may be only twenty-one, but
He taught us, eye to eye.

Forever Story

How many times have we wished to be able to stay in one particular place because it was so exquisitely perfect, beautiful and filled with serenity and peace? Remember the sigh, the soft moan, and the feeling of awe that you experienced in the precise moment. It is the place of complete and absolute inspiration. It is the place where artists, lovers, and people of all faiths create. It is the place where photographs, paintings, lyrical notes, and writings of extraordinary value are birthed. It is the place where God opens the door of perfection to the future of unending joy, and the vision of what is waiting for those who believe. We are held captive in time to see, to recognize, to acknowledge, and finally, to express the supernatural gift from God in human form. It comes from the Lord, Himself, as He gives us the ability to record through a visual or auditory revelation the phenomenal power of the Almighty God! So what holds us spellbound? Consider the sky, the sunrise, the sunset, the mountaintops, the ocean, the rainbow, the clouds, the lush valley of flowers, the endless streams and brooks, the cliffs, the rain forest, the plants, the trees, the glaciers, the arctic, the atmosphere, the universe, and all that stretches for millions of miles above and all that flows deep beneath us for endless miles below. These visions, more simply put, are props from God that have inspired artists and people who never saw themselves as artists, to expound and enrich the lives and hearts of the hungry, the needy, and those who long to feel life.

These awe-inspiring gifts are the prelude of a heavenly life, and the cataclysmic explosion of joy that will be bestowed on us when at last we meet the Maker of these divine inspirations that have blessed our eyes for untold years. Most of us have fallen to our knees, slid to the ground, or quietly stood in absolute wonder of these incredible visions given to us at the prepared times in our walk. Can you imagine the joy of living in the fantastic dream that your entire being, is mesmerized and held captive to? What if you could fly through the clouds, breathe beneath the sea, live in the valley of exotic flowers, rest in the warmth of the sunset, sleep floating in the atmosphere, walk on a star, communicate with all God's creatures, feel life in every living thing? What if you could stay forever in that perfect awe-inspiring moment when peace is all you know.

Well, for me, I would stand in the sunset. But each of you has your own special place. Think of your place, because though it will be different from mine, I believe it shares one commonality. Our places each respectively lead us to His face; the Creator, the God of every living thing, with a sweep of His hand created your vision, perfectly planned. Oh family of His---He wants you to revel in those times; paint them, photograph them, sing them, write them, but most of all, He wants you to live them! Live them in hope believing that someday you will be surrounded with every vision of beauty that He has so graciously presented to us, though fleeting, but most assuredly eternally ours someday. So dear one, for now, just bask in the fantastic endeavor! Understand that we cannot live in the sunrise or the sunset here on earth, but briefly. Still, He sends the visions so we can anticipate, then see, His creation of the prelude, the introduction to: FOREVER.

Forever

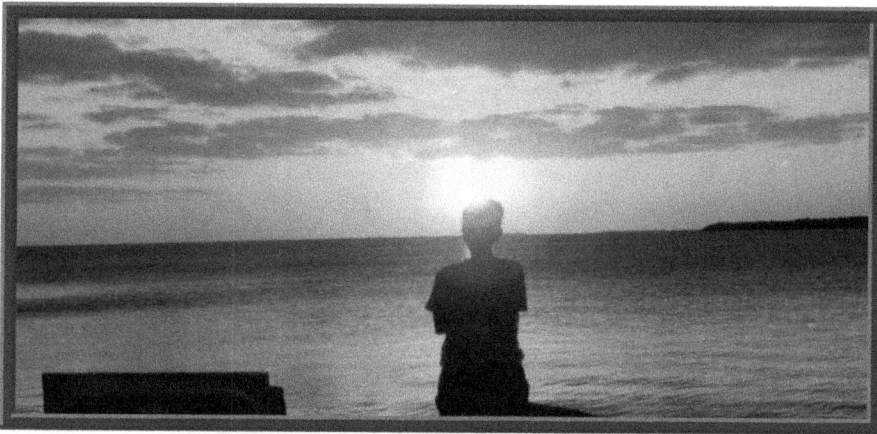

Not an artist known to many
But words come without fanfare
Not a singer or musical genius
Yet He gives these words to share.

Mesmerizing visions, stunning
Granted to me, a simple soul
The awe-inspiring words of hope
God speaks, perpetuates the goal.

But would I stand paralyzed?
By this mind altering sight
Then keep it selfishly to myself
And not long; long to write?

Breath-taking panoramic visions
Silent scenes beneath the sea
These gifts bombard my senses
A prelude to life, God gives to me.

Life, a life with our Father
To stand in the sunset, true?
Or live in an awe-inspiring moment
Witness this: to live my life with You.

These visions, though brief, are real
My heart pounds with each endeavor
Fantastic sights, inexplicably mine, then
Walks me into Your arms---Forever.

Forevermore

I dreamed the last dance in my heart
From the echoes of a song I shall depart
Not to leave my loved ones here to cry
I am singing joyfully up on high.

I dreamed the first dance with my true love
The Father God my Savior from above
From the echoes of the song I sing anew
The last dance now begins my life with You.

The last dance now remembered on this earth
But His music called to me from my birth
The gifts that I have shared for all these years
May bring to some a melody of tears.

I dreamed the last dance in my heart
As God had choreographed it from the start
Look to the heavens though it may seem far
See me dance the last dance on a star.

Singing for the one that I adored
My voice lifts up in praise to my Lord
The last dance thru the glory of heaven's door
I dance at last with Him forevermore...

∾∾

In loving memory of Donna Summer

Friend Story

It is no small thing to be friends with God. This is surely an understatement, because to be His friend, is HUGE! You will find yourself in complete wonder when the absoluteness of eternity with Him becomes a solid fact. I am friends with God! He sent me His request long ago. It is with deep humiliation that I admit to not clicking on the "accept" button at the precise moment when He asked for my friendship. But we are certainly in some amazing times when half the world is clicking away and acknowledging a total stranger that precious gift of the "yes" and accept their "friendship." One might ask, is this really a surprising phenomenon? I am friends with so and so because they said they are friends with this one person I do know. Yes, I do know the person so I click yes to you, and now you have access to my life, my personal thoughts, my dreams, and the intimate details of my heart. I said "yes" to you.

In the beginning, I believed this was a marvelous way to express my love for God, family and friends. It was a delightful conduit to the world and to so many who live in far off places. However, there can be naiveté's about opening up ones heart to the vast numbers. Bear with me in this quote: "Good things come in small packages." Yesterday I received a small package from a dear friend. It was an old book in mint condition, but most importantly, it was filled with lovely and unexpected poetry. Here are my thoughts. The size/smallness of the gift spoke volumes of the hugeness of the friendship! Please humor me with another quote: "Do you think money grows on trees?" Oh, I have said this to my children on countless occasions. Now again if you will, here is my quote: "Friends do not grow on Facebook." It is the exact opposite. Facebook can grow through the thoughtfulness of friends. I was able to feel this yesterday when an avalanche of well wishes came to me on my birthday. Can I tell you that a large portion of the wishes came from people that I have never met, but have grown to know their hearts through the many conversations over the past few years? Most likely we will never meet in this life, because they live so far away, some in countries I barely heard of. So, what is the purpose of all this? At first the social networking was fun and delightful. Then a few years later the communications I noticed between people stunned me. The dialogue was becoming openly hurtful. Young people especially, would use language that would have served me a bar of Ivory soap for my main meal if Facebook existed when I was a teen. OK, let's go back a few paragraphs when I said, "I clicked 'yes' to you and now you have access to my life, my personal thoughts, and the intimate details of my heart." I said "yes" to you! This is a perfect allegory. You first asked me-you first liked me-finally; I said "yes"! Here is the lesson I learned this morning: I am friends with God because He was first friends with me. He first loved me! This was no accident. This was a deliberate and direct request from God. He wanted to be my friend. I have given up bemoaning the fact that I waited so long to accept His friendship and now simply revel in His love. How precious and marvelous is that! I pray not to lose sight of what God longs to share with me. You see, I have been feeling sorry for myself. Don't be surprised. You have been there too. Facebook has made it possible to reach out and verbally smack someone! I have seen these supposedly "wisdom-filled" decorated word boxes that reek of passive-aggressive word slams! Please, let me say first hand that I am guilty and have fallen prey to these wordy little pieces because it is an easy way to make one's feelings known in a seemingly nice way. Now here is the question of the day. Why do we love Facebook? For me, it is the personal connection and the photos that allow me to be part of the lives of those I love. This surely is a good thing and once again, thank you for allowing me to be your friend, because you clicked the "yes" and I am truly grateful for that. Now I pray that in this upcoming year, I can avoid the little nuances of words that are not pleasing to my best friend. For it is no small thing to be friends with God!

In closing, dear friends, as I pondered Mother's Day and the birthday I wished to avoid, I reached down for that little book that my fingers have been itching to open when my phone rang. I looked at my caller ID and instant tears came. An old friend was calling. In that moment God must have smiled because this is the ONLY friend I have that has not succumbed to Facebook, texting, iPad, iPod, and the iPhone. She just remained, "iFriend." This is my newly created word, and absolutely everyone should have an iFriend! We talked long and intimately; and that was God's gift to me before I closed my eyes on the day that I turned sixty-four. She made me long to turn back the hands of time, when we sat next to each other in church and whispered during the teaching, like little girls; except when Scott was teaching! On those nights she made me think of the tears we cried as we shared a damp tissue. She made me think of our trips to the Zoo (which gives me a belly laugh as I write)! She made me think of the day we spent on the ocean when she caught all the fish. She made me think of the fabulous meals she prepared in her home as we sat and ate and watched the sun set on the lake. She made me think of the U Miami Basketball games that she bought tickets for us, and we screamed until we were hoarse. She made me think of the day she let me pretend that her classic Corvette convertible was mine, and she even took a photo of me in the driver's seat! She made me think of those most profound and deeply spiritual teachings from a man of God who connects us as more than friends, but as family. He knows who he is, my precious brother in Christ. She made me miss him as we lingered on him to have bragging rights as he is her son-in-law and I am his sister. She made me think of his humility and so I shall not write his name. Oh, I could go on and on here, but I shall just say the absolute best part of having this woman for my friend is: she made me think, period. She made me think...

Most of you know a poem will follow this story. I could write a book about this woman, but instead I pulled from my shelf my very first book of poetry that was published titled, *So Close to God.* There is no denying the wonder and beauty of my friend that is written about on page 118 in my first published book. In 2007, God gave me poetic verses to be shared about friendship. Her friendship has touched me, blessed me, taught me, and tonight brought these memories to my mind. Though we live miles apart, she remains close inside my heart; memories of a woman that shall never end. In sweet wonder now and always, Gayle, I call you, Friend...

Friend

I always see compassion
Looking back at me
When I look into your eyes
It's all that I can see.

A thoughtful look
A gentle touch
A warmth that's true
And means so much.

I always see a loving heart
Looking back at me
When I look into your eyes
It's all that I can see.

A tender smile
An encouraging word
A firm hug
I'm reassured.

I always see wisdom
Looking back at me
When I look into your eyes
It's all that I can see.

A precious moment
Full of sisterly love
A friend indeed
From Him above.

I always see a spiritual truth
Looking back at me
When I look into your eyes
It's all that I can see.

I always see a reflection
Looking back at me
When I look into your eyes
I pray like you I'll be.

From Here To There Story

*Written expressly for Cheri Reese,
Funeral Director Lane Mineral Ridge Chapel*

She sat on my couch next to me. On her lap, she held the remains of my husband in a small box. I felt comforted by her presence as she explained to me what she was about to do. Even though I was prepared by Cheri for this moment, it still swept my breath away when she opened the box and inside was a plastic bag filled with a white powdery substance; that was all that remained of my precious Jim. Then, she took both of my hands, and placed them on his cremated remains. In an instant, I went from here to there. The essence of Jim's earthly body was in my hands, but his spirit was with God. Someday, someday, so shall I be---there.

To go from here to there, may seem impossible. This lovely woman was given a holy gift, and with deep compassion and kindness, she helps the brokenhearted take that giant leap of faith. So few are given this most angelic work. I am thankful to God for Cheri Reese. She is a beautiful person, not only spiritually, but also intellectually. For whatever one's spiritual belief, Cheri walks that person through the saddest moment in their life.

Cheri is a Funeral Director, and an angel and protector of life after death. These are my perceptions, as one who has had the great honor of experiencing who she is and how passionately and with incredible humility, she gives her heart to this work. I am in awe of how very much she would care. And in that most intimate moment, Cheri took me---from here to there…

ೂ

Blessed are those who mourn, For they shall be comforted.

Matthew 5:4 (NKJV)

Photo credit Kent Viklund.

30

From Here To There

Beside me rests a book I dare to read
It speaks of life and death, where it might lead
So often the last breath leaves one unprepared
But the Father sends an angel, for He so cared.

The absence of life brings a shuddering silence
Until the words of His servant softly commence
This holy work bears an inexplicable sorrow
As shattered hearts try to imagine tomorrow.

There is great love for this work to be done
For it cannot be done by just anyone
But this one possesses a desire within her soul
To comfort a broken heart that was once whole.

In that time when pain will crush the spirit
Through gut wrenching tears this one will sit
Until the perfect moment she will direct and protect
And from her heart peace comes with utmost respect.

So, we are here, but someday, we'll be—there
Only God knows of the when and where
His angel stands vigil to help the weary see
That with our loved ones someday, we shall be.

This work will be gifted to only a certain few
As God speaks and teaches what they must do
With great dignity and kindness she breathes a prayer
Then carries those entrusted to her; from here to there.

৵৩

We are confident, yes, well pleased rather
to be absent from the body and to be present with the Lord.
Corinthians 5:8 (NKJV)

Give Her More Story

Over thirty years ago I wondered if there was a God, and there were times when leaving this world seemed a credible option when I was so tired of the fight. Not really knowing who God was, kept me very low. When I was thirty-four, a thyroid cancer that was supposedly cured came back in my neck's lymph nodes. My husband, and father of my children, wanted a divorce. My Dad died suddenly of a heart attack, and I was working two jobs to support my family. My children and Mom were devastated. There was one particular night that took me to a place of such despair; grief swept over me. I simply did not want to be there or anywhere. It was just a brief moment in time. I imagine it was that very dark place where some go tragically to the end of life as we know it. At some point, there was a surrendering and the desperation of my depression brought me to the morning with a prayer. I asked God for time. I just wanted to raise my son and daughter. "Let me live until they graduate from high school," I said. Now, I smile at my lack of understanding in this request, not knowing who God was---I wish to thank Him for not answering that prayer as requested, because He gave me more, when I asked for less! It is now over thirty years since that prayer, and twenty-plus years beyond my time requested! God had good plans for me, according to Jeremiah 29:11. I wonder how many have lowered their standards in their prayer life. It took eighteen years after that fateful night of decision to live or not to live, to forgive or not to forgive, that brought me to Who God is. Since then, my life is no longer about living, but it is about giving. I gave my pitiful heart to Christ. However, the surrender has not stopped the trials, but it has stopped the struggle. My God, my Savior, my Father stands before me, beside me, and behind me. Life is hard, but life before Christ, was almost unbearable. Imagine the revelation that comes after all these years! He gave me more when I asked for less!

If you are my friend, then you know that I seldom mention dealing with cancer when I was thirty-two years old. It was not the worst part of my life. The worst part of my life was losing those I loved and having no one to turn to with my heartache and fear. I was completely lost. If you are wondering why I am writing today about a seemingly healed scar from long ago, allow me to explain. Recently, I met a young mother. She is only thirty-eight years old. She has three young children. Within a six-month period of time, her Mom died, her husband was killed in a tragic accident and she gave birth to a baby girl. During the C-section delivery of her baby, aggressive ovarian cancer was discovered. She has had many surgeries and battled for her life for three and a half years. When I first met Danielle and her three girls, I was stunned by her beauty and poise. I could see how very sick she was. Yet, we cried together, prayed together, and when we hugged good-bye she asked me to bring her a Bible. She shares with me her desire to raise her children; but the chemotherapy has taken away the desire to fight. She is weak and in constant pain. I do not blame her for being tired of the fight, but God is sending in His troops. I told Danielle about my life thirty years ago and how God did not answer my prayer as asked. I am still here, and miraculously, God is my center, my hope, and my life. This precious woman is in a fight and our God is able! I prayed with her for more time, but most of all that she would allow the Comforter to hold her tight. Oh yes, this woman is in a fight and she says, "I need a Bible" and this I can manage for sure, but it will be God who gives her strength and courage and hope to endure. Father today I cry to You as she opens up the door; give her more...

Give Her More

Photo credit: Gloria Dingeldein

It is often the things of life
That we are not prepared for
It's the shock of another's heartache
That brings us to Your door
The answer is not always clear
Tears fall from the eyes of this one
Her pain breaks our hearts again
This battle we pray to be won.

It is often the things of life
That leaves us completely undone
Drags us through a pain wracked day
Then lies down with the setting sun
This is the fate of a precious soul
That stirs a godly person to pray
Against the savageness of the disease
That comes to steal the time away.

It is often the things of life
That brings us heavily to our knees
In a state so weakened, we cry
Weeping, help me, help me, please
Yet in those moments of suffering
When darkness pressed cold with fear
In those times of surrendering
That's when Our Lord draws near.

It is often the things of life
When the spirit, too weary to weep
Though silent and broken cry to God
Then before Him drift off to sleep
But my Lord had heard my plea
Even though I asked for less
He gave me more, gave me more
Because my Father God longs to bless.

God Breathed Story

Every morning upon awakening, I reach for a stack of books; my Bible, devotionals, and my notebook begin my day. There is hope that God would have a word with me. Today I am reading the summer edition of **Words of Life Devotional** that contains some writings that I contributed. One might find it strange that I am surprised by the content. This morning as in every morning when awareness comes, there is a need. There is a need to pray, meditate, and try to understand the reason for the circumstances of life. So my eyes pass over sentence after sentence in this devotional, and now, I am amazed by the good humor and generosity of God. There is a hope-filled treasure of God-inspired writings, sharing His Empirical Word!

Now if it were truly up to me to write this book it would not be a treasure of hope. It would be what the youth of today call, "a hot mess!" Yes, "hot mess" is the phrase rage of today. But, my age and experience would give me this word to describe what life would be like without God. Not, "hot mess," well maybe, but most assuredly the word "clueless" comes to mind. You see, as I read this devotional that literally has my name on every other page, a shocking realization comes! I don't remember writing these words that seem to fall into place and now in a quiet moment of grace, I understand what God-inspired means. God's Word, His Holy Scriptures, were written by those He chose; none-the-less it was His words written for us through mere men. So what then?

When we as Christians hear this proclamation from others: "Men wrote the Bible;" sometimes it sets me down as I reach deep into my own spirituality to relate and prayerfully not to confound. It is hard to grasp the phrase "God-inspired" in myself. Then comes God-breathed and God said, "Write this down!" On this particular morning, I write before I pray. Words come in a divine and unexpected way. So I write, never knowing what God will say. Finally, when the words cease to flow---I suspect God smiles and off He will go. Now I read these words in complete wonder knowing I had been blessed into a most incredible spiritual high, not understanding why. Write, write, write, yes, but know this; it was not I. Well then, we certainly understand "hot mess' and we understand "clueless" and I will say here and now that God has never failed me, as He has left, or if you will allow me to say, "bequeathed" and honored me with these treasured words---God-breathed...

രുള

All Scripture is God-breathed and is useful for teaching, rebuking, correcting and training in righteousness, so that the servant of God may be thoroughly equipped for every good work.
2 Timothy 3:16-17 (NIV)

God Breathed

Photo Credit: Judy A. Bauman

Read, inhale His words
Treasured and hoped for
Take in, claim, yours
God, God give us more.

Oh Lord, why now?
For who am I?
That You would bequeath
Into me and breathe?

Your words on this page
On mornings crystal clear
Write, write, write, yes!
Words audible to hear?

No, but inspired by Him
Words churned and seethed
Holy and sweetly given
To me—God-Breathed…

God Talks To Me Story

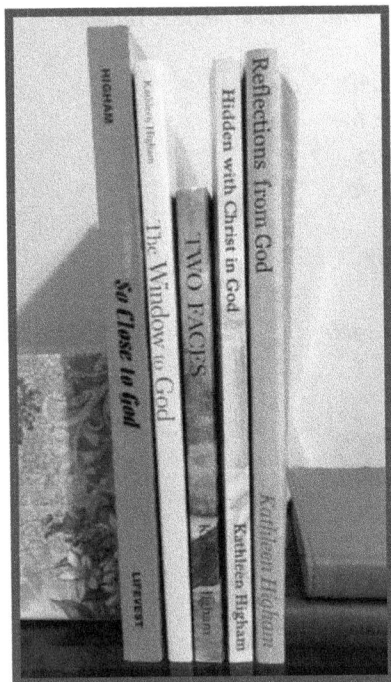

In one day, God spoke to me on several issues. I read, "You must turn your thoughts and your eyes away from the face of idols and look to Him and be saved (see Isaiah 45:22)" from *My Utmost For His Highest* (Chambers, February 11, Is Your Mind Stayed in God?). Then, in the same devotional by Oswald Chambers, he stated, "When you have thoughts and ideas that are worthy of credit to God, learn to compare and associate them with all that happen in nature- the rising and setting of the sun…" I just wrote a devotional and poem called, *Early Morning* about the rising and setting sun. I continued reading in Chambers' devotional, "Then prod your memory and wake up immediately. Don't say to yourself, 'But God is not talking to me right now.' He ought to be."

Later, on this same day a lovely man, a musician, sent me a song he recorded from a poem that I wrote called, *Look Up*. Shortly thereafter, I received an email from a woman I have never met about a poem I posted on Facebook. She wrote: "Our God talks to you for real!!!" Well, there is no doubt that God talks to me and I ponder these words He gives. I am ever mindful of the words that seep inside my soul, and from my lips I speak in wonder, "Oh my, His Spirit lives!"

God Talks To Me

Oh my, His Spirit lives!
Writing words through my soul
Seeps into the unattainable part
Speaks to me, makes me whole.

He writes for me, He surely does
So amazed when His words came
As I write them down in awe
Then honor them in a frame.

Incredibly, He gives this gift
Words between the cover of a book
His Holy thoughts, He shares
If you will, come take a look.

Oh my, His Spirit lives!
Words, His words for all to see
In a poem, a book, a song, a prayer
So divinely, God talks to me.

He Is Faithful Story

This was written during a most difficult week, some years ago, when Jim had been in the hospital with an unstoppable nose bleed. He had a very rough five days as a balloon was inflated in his nose causing him extreme pain. He had to get four units of plasma before a procedure was done to stop the bleeding. He had a procedure in interventional radiology called embolization. Stents were placed in the nasal vessels that were bleeding and the blood flow was blocked. The balloon was deflated and the procedure was successful. We came home late in the afternoon and he was exhausted and feeling a little poorly. It was most likely due to the stress of severe pain, blood loss, and strong pain medications. I expected him to improve with each day. However, I will confess to you my fear and anguish throughout this week. I wish I could say I was a stellar Christian completely trusting in God. I was not. I was terrified and absolutely heartbroken to watch Jim suffer so much. Here is the good news. Even while I was unbelieving, my God was faithful! Life will progress or regress, but no matter what, God is faithful!

Recently, I learned of a precious new friend that was sent home with hospice care to live the remainder of her life. She was only thirty-eight and she has a family she would love to raise. My heart breaks for this woman who is a child of God. As we prayed for time for her, once again, God is faithful. Her story makes our story inconsequential. I ask all of you dear friends to pray for Danielle's family, for whatever God has planned for them. I pray to simply know that even when we can't believe, He is faithful!

He Is Faithful

There can be no birth without pain
Yet we shall plunge forward still
Striving for a life unknown in awe
Praying the moments not to be in vain.

Oft we falter because we are weak
Frail and lost we may flounder
Fickle human beings cry to Him again
Frightened souls on a journey, seek.

But our God, so faithful is He
Understands the failings of His flock
His hand touches every heart that breaks
Says, "Come all who are weary, come to me."

Yes, pain, sorrow, grief, and unbelief
Might attack those who belong to Him
But even in our weakness He is there
The Comforter longs to bring relief.

There can be no birth without pain
On those days we cannot believe
Remember He is faithful, never to deny
His purpose, the reason He was slain.

On this day no matter how fateful
He cannot deny Himself
Especially when we believe not
He abideth faithful!

❧❧

If we believe not, yet he abideth faithful:
He cannot deny himself. **2 Timothy 2:13 (KJV)**

Heroes Story

It is human nature to have these moments, these times when we doubt our choices and the place where life has taken us. Fear and uncertainty can erode self-confidence as maturity finds the back door. Even getting out of bed can become a chore. Life is not what we expected. Compassion and passion wanes. Friends seem far away. Family, well family, will most always be there, but time is still slipping away. So, who do you look too? In whom have you placed your hope? When I was small, my hero was my Dad. When he died, my hero became my Mom until I became a teenager, and then my hero became that guy. That guy became the husband who walked away. My bruised heart could only hope to be the hero for my children. I am sure I fell short there. When they grew up, the job and my social life became my source of joy. My adventures, travels, running, and constantly looking for new experiences were often my focus. My focus was intensified by me. My motto: I can do anything! And, I did do everything, every chance I got. So who was my hero, really? It was me! I pleased myself, collected some wonderful friends along the way, and I must acknowledge their worth and value in my life. Yet, I had not found what I was looking for. There came a time when I realized that I had my family, friends, good health, a home, a job with some measure of success, but an empty gnawing ache in my heart remained. Whenever there was disappointment or pain, there was always someone else to blame. Until one day, my Mom, my hero, who kept me grounded, quietly passed away. There was no warning, no chance to hug her again, no chance to laugh and cry with her; no chance to tell her that I longed to be like her, that I challenged my entire being to have a fraction of her character and courage. There was no second chance and it hit me with a devastating force that dropped me and emptied me of life and peace. I had absolutely no hope. When I remember those days it is clear to me that every person I came close to was a potential hero. I cried and raged at God, yet still I could not see. The true hero was not my Dad, my Mom, and especially not me. The true hero was He---The One who gave me life.

Over twelve years ago, God, my Father, came into my heart and awakened the deadness in my soul. He dwells in me. He makes me whole. So, who is your hero? Who is the one being that is never going to leave, never going to fail? Do you even know? Can you surrender and let go? If you do, God will bring hope to you, maybe with a little help from a friend. The friend you thought you knew was sent by Him to teach, to instruct, to guide, and most importantly to give honor and glory to the One who loves unconditionally. Because we often struggle with the gift of loving without expecting something in return, God frequently sends more than one to help us. I have lost count of those precious souls that have carried me through the battle field of life. Who is your true hero? Do you even know? This morning, I read this from one of my devotionals. *My Utmost for His Highest*, "This is the firm and immovable secret of the Lord to those who trust Him—'I will give your life to you . . . .'" (Chambers, April 28).

Abandon yourself and just let go! Feel your heart melt when at last you know. It is God who sends them. But only God is your true Hero…

Heroes

Long ago life was good to me
Dad rocked me gently on his knee
No worries ever, that I could see
Time with them was always carefree.

One sunny morn Dad passed away
Life changed forever on that day
My Mom, my hero carried us all
She knew every time I would fall.

Still, life was good to me
I married and began a family
But the man simply walked away
Again, life changed forever on that day.

Oh, I could hardly bear the sight
My hero slipped silently into the night
God! I raged and cried, "This isn't right!"
She left me alone in this fight.

No longer was life good to me
And no more heroes could I see
Many friends came and lovers too
Yet, I would not turn to You.

I traversed the mountains to the sea
Traveled the world—who could it be?
Pain, sorrow, and grief forged ahead
My heavy heart beat with dread.

Still, I would not surrender to You
I didn't even know what to do
Until a friend helped with the search
Drove to me to this lovely little church.

Hope—hope was what I longed for
It waited patiently behind that door
Love embraced me, my heart would soar
As life looked back at me once more.

Sweetly they stood there—the two heroes
Where they came from, well, God knows
This elderly couple prayed to intercede
My heart surrendered, at last was freed.

Now life has surely been good to me
When all of His heroes came to be
For He had sent them, this I know
But only God is my true Hero...

◈◈

Sometimes I need to write the moment of completion when God gives me proof of His absolute love for me. This morning I wrote this piece about heroes, but after I wrote the devotional and poem I picked up my favorite book and read the very first line. It is from **Streams in the Desert**: "God is continually preparing His heroes and when the opportunity is right, He puts them into position in an instant. He works so fast, the world wonders where they came from." (April 28, Cowman and Reimann). I don't know why I am so surprised when God verifies His blessing on me... One could say that is what heroes do...Allow me to now share the poem that was written along with this message.

Human strength and human greatness
Spring not from life's sunny side
Heroes must be more than driftwood
Floating on a waiting tide.

(**Streams in the Desert,** April 28, Cowman and Reimann).
◈◈

Every year as we approach Mother's Day I begin to write the story in my head. This year I wanted to bury my head in the sand (Hawaii would have been nice). Mother's Day is coming and it will be fifteen years since I last shared this day with my Mom. This Mother's Day happens to fall on my birthday. I will be turning 65! But, I shall keep my head held up high, because it would not honor her to whine about my age. She was the grandest hero that God put into my life. So, for my Mom, and all of you who have carried me to this place, I say, "Thank you for your greatness, your sunny side, and that you would drift away with me on the waiting tide. It has been a remarkable and most marvelous ride..."

His Story

When I sign a book or note to someone, I always write, "His," then I sign my name. I am so thankful that I am "His." There are times of wonder that He would want me, but He does, and I am indeed, "His." But, even though I know that I belong to Him, I still try to make my own moves now and then. The outcome never changes, because when I make decisions without God, the usual confusion and disruption roars back into my life. Stress, anxiety, and fear rob me of my peace. Because we are human we can easily slip back, believing we can take control. Well, stress, anxiety, and fear are three emotions that I want to give completely to God. It is absolutely exhausting to venture into that place of utter chaos. Yet, I am "His." I pray that I will never again see these things that so burden me. On this Resurrection Day, I raise my hand to Him in praise; to the One who set me free. Now, I sit quietly and He sits quietly beside me. I am "His…"

His

Even when I sit quietly
Without Him comes anxiety
Hiding in my heart, stressed
A fear of silent evil rests.
Yet, I am "His."

Even when I sit quietly
My sorrow no one else can see
The pain buried deep inside
Holds me tight, peace denied.
Still, I am "His."

Even when I sit quietly
It doesn't mean that I am free
Until I give to God complete control
And every burden within my soul.
Then, I am "His."

Even when I sit quietly
Raise my hand for all to see
God will come so mercifully
For He sits quietly beside me.
Now, I am "His."

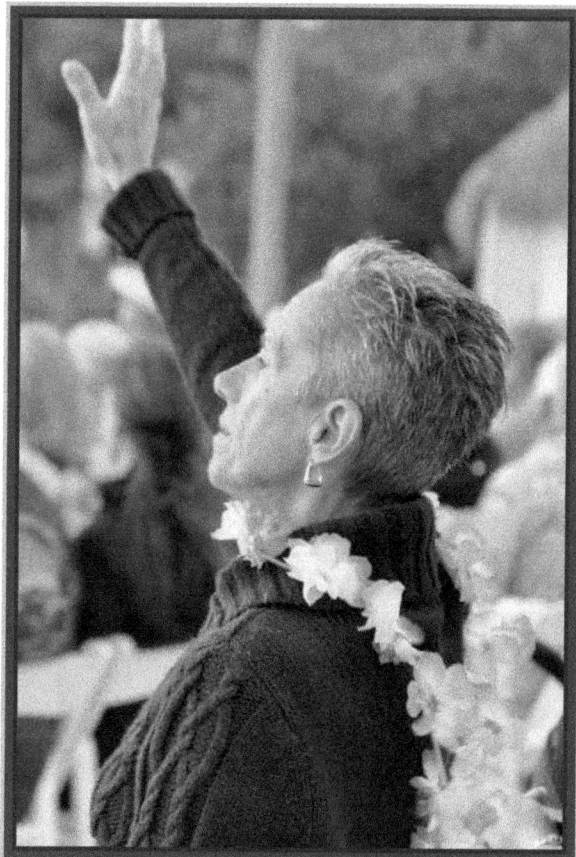

Photo Credit: Kathleen Denis

41

Heroes-Healers Story

Healers, doctors, nurses and medical servants; never cease to amaze me. Let me first just say thank you to all of those who work on the sixth floor of HMHP and have spent much of their time in room 6521 taking care of Jim. You excelled beyond the call of duty and I cannot express how much Jim and I appreciate each and every one of you!

Because my husband had multiple health issues, I have been witness to the genius of the healer. I call them heroes because of who they are and how they serve. If you know me, then you know how often I write about physicians. There is one who I have been waiting to write about. She is one of many heroes who will come and go fleetingly, as needed, in and out of our lives. There is no question of her genius and her complete dedication to her patients. All who know her, have a respect and a desire to reach the higher standard that she first holds herself accountable at every moment that she is serving. She is a formidable presence that causes one to want to excel. But beneath her genius, which is so extraordinary, lies a hero.

She is a woman who works hard, and spends endless hours helping her very sick patients. I believe I have never written about her because my words could not do justice to who she really is. Jim and I privately call her our "Princess." When she comes into our room we feel surrounded by peace, truth, trust and honesty.

We have had the privilege of knowing this woman on a professional level as a revered physician for many years. As this past week was winding down, and I wondered if she ever rests. She is our doctor, our princess, our genius, and above all, she is our humble servant. She is as the lamb, and at the same time, she will fight like a lion for those who are in her care. She serves with a firm and prayerful heart that places her patients above everything. When she walks onto the unit, things happen, people move, awareness explodes. She seeks perfection in her quest for healing.

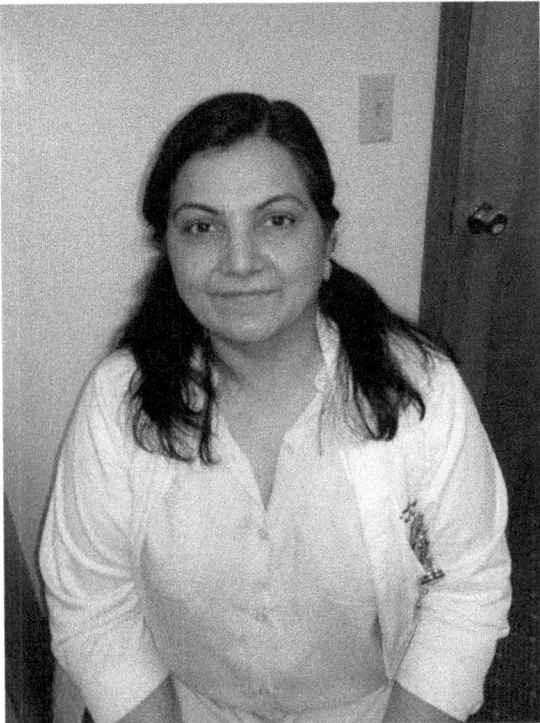

When I see her strolling down the hall, I feel safe just, because she is close by. Thank you for allowing a very simple soul like me to see into your beautiful compassionate heart and incomprehensible brain. You are gifted by God to be one of the most amazing healers! We pray for you to know how much we value, appreciate, and love who you are---princess, hero, healer! Thank you, Dr. Mita Raheja!

Heroes-Healers

Day by day, I watched these gifted ones
Heroes, sometimes even when they fell
Now I lacked the knowledge to understand
So, I followed them down the well.

Fear dark and ferocious came to me
Tried to think and study to no avail
Impossible, impossible, I cried again!
But my hero as always, she would prevail.

A battle drained the body, but not the soul
Praising God for all that He would give
Succumbing to that which is divine
Remembering how He wants me to live.

First and always the heroes are His
And He gave them extraordinary power
So very close, they touch with holiness
Draw on His genius in that hour.

Lay hands, hearts, minds and spirituality
Upon a body prostrate before their eyes
But a common man will never understand
How God honors these capable to mesmerize.

Day by day I watched these gifted ones
Draw on the power of God alone
With lightning speed He answers them
Seeds of life into their minds are sown.

Dear Lord, we thank you for the heroes
Whose brilliance humbly follows Your way
Up from the well and through another day
Oh, amazing healers, for you, I pray.

❧❧

Let them give thanks
to the LORD for his unfailing love
and his wonderful deeds for mankind,
Psalm 107:8 (NIV)

I Am Close To God Story

Here is something to ponder. When God blesses me, I am enthralled and filled with abounding joy. My thankfulness is sincere in the moment. I am close to God. When life frightens me, I frantically and aggressively cry out to Him to deliver me and protect me from evil. My request is sincere in the moment. I am close to God. When I awaken in the morning, I praise Him and ask for His blessings. My heart is sincere in the moment. I am close to God. When at night, I fall fast asleep, my soul rests quietly and I know God is close to me.

My ponderings are surely not of thankfulness for the countless blessings or my relief for His protection and certainly not my complete peace when He watches over me as I sleep. My pondering is: what happens in-between those times when extreme awareness, such as the polar opposites of joy and fear are absent, and also when slumber, which is the essence of being unaware, present? What happens in the lull, where mundane moments come, and we seek Him not? For this has been a very long cold winter. It has been fraught with wind and snow, and in-between, comes mud puddles.

I wonder and ponder if these moments are turning points of apathy unbeknownst to us, the slithering ugliness of tepidity and insensitivity that can take hold of those who live in the moment, but lack the fervor of the extreme and become a tenant in a place of complacency. There would be no need to thank or ask and no desire to move into the peaceful rest of Christ, because they are neither hot nor cold, but have settled for lukewarm. This is a place I call flat. There is no hill up or down, twisting around. It is flat, expressionless and void. This is not a place where I wish to be.

There is duplicity in that one can speak one way in times of blessing, and one way in times of protection, and then, not speak at all---in the lull. The lull can become insidiously dangerous if one does not guard the heart; the heart that belongs to God. Our God will allow us to listen to our heart, and that is good for those who have asked Him in. He is there, and even when He is silent, we must not be silent in regards to speaking to Him. When we become silent, the lull creeps in.

This morning, I pondered these moments of stillness, knowing He is there. Though the lull tempts and pulls, it cannot tempt the love of God or pull us from His grasp. The lull is empty, yet full of evil. Thank God, it will not last. The duplicity of the lull is that it is empty, and at the same time, it is full of nothing worthy of thought. Until you call on Him who tramples the lull beneath His feet, and in the moment, you and the mud puddle meet. Be sincere and wait for the ripple to settle. See your murky reflection of laughter and do not to think it odd when you hear yourself say, "I am close to God."

ॐॐ

Draw near to God and He will draw near to you.
James 4:8a (NKJV)

I Am Close To God

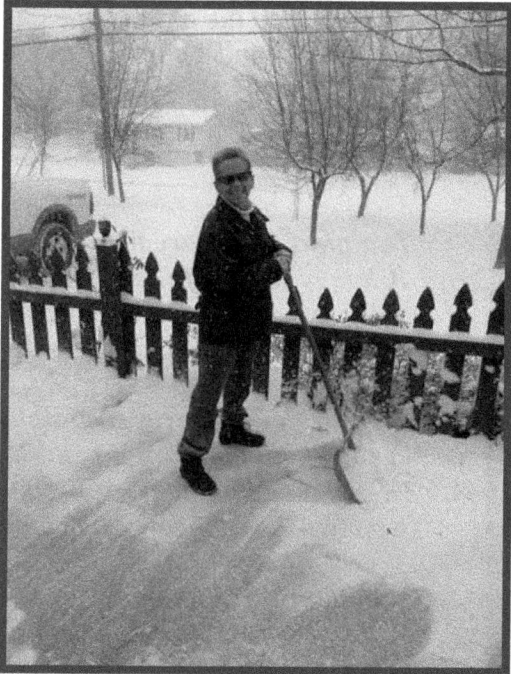

Should I detest the winter?
Cringe as the wind will blow
Balk and shiver in disgust
At the piling up of snow.

It is not strange to ponder
When in the blustering cold I huddle
And in the lull stare and search
For my reflection in the mud puddle.

When the ripples of the puddle settle
Laughter bursts out in simplicity
Snow, wind, sludge and mud, yet
In me there is no duplicity.

Peace comes in the moment
And I do not think it odd
Peace comes as I speak these words
"I am close to God."

❧❧

"For as the heavens are higher than the earth,
So are My ways higher than your ways,
And My thoughts than your thoughts.
"For as the rain comes down, and the snow from heaven,
And do not return there, But water the earth,
And make it bring forth and bud,
That it may give seed to the sower
And bread to the eater,
So shall My word be that goes forth from My mouth;
It shall not return to Me void,
But it shall accomplish what I please,
And it shall prosper in the thing for which I sent it.
Isaiah 55:9-11 (NKJV)

Hold Me Story

A precious friend confided in me, that one night, she felt filled with despair. She lay in her bed unable to say or do anything, but in that moment she whispered to God, "Please hold me." Then, my friend tells me that a white light filled the air and she could feel Him holding her. Oh, if only we could ask Him, knowing and believing that He would…

Hold Me

Tonight I lay weary in my bed
A heavy sorrow fills my head
I do not want to feel this way
There are no words that I can say.

Still and rigid my eyes shut tight
No sleep will come on this night
The silence in a heart of dread
My body weighted down like lead.

I would cry, but I simply cannot
A losing battle if I had fought
Then I felt Him, could it be?
From my lips I say, "Hold me."

God hold me, hold me please
Unable to fall upon my knees
It hurts too much to even try
But the white light came to defy.

He held me with the softest sigh
And for just a moment I did cry
Understanding this to be a test
Now in His arms at last, I rest.

So ask Him in a that time of need
From every burden you are freed
If only you can say, "Hold me"
He would, just ask, ask and see.

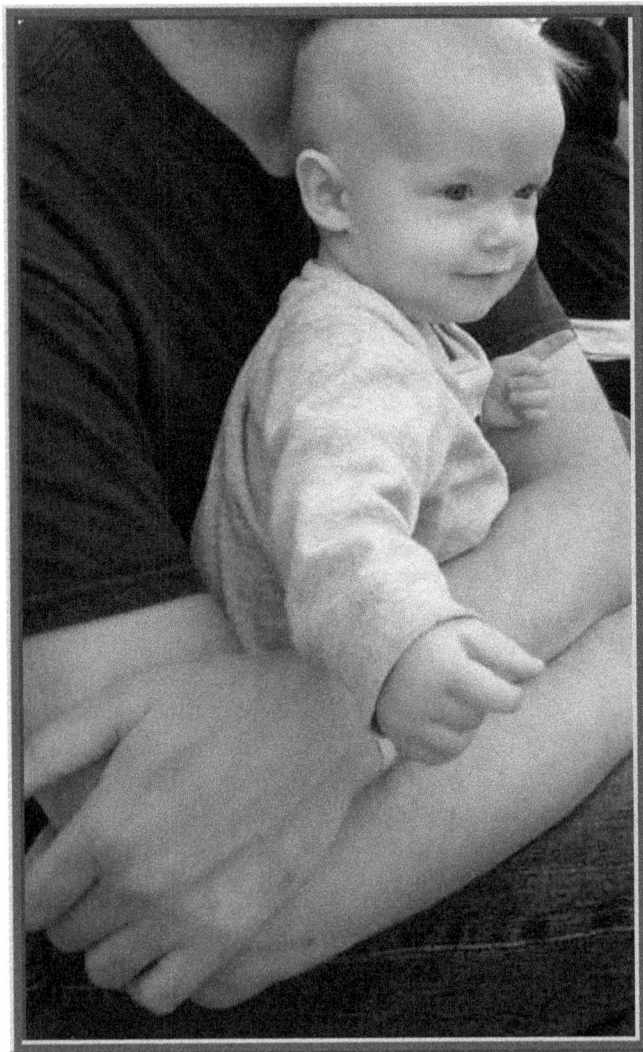

Photo credit: Kent Viklund

I Am Here Story

Even God does not create a glorious sunset without zest. It is an artful masterpiece that paints the sky unto the West. Then, down in absolute silence, the glow shall crest. I am in love with the end of the day; knowing God is with me, come what may. My eyes close in wonder of what is yet to come, or if my eyes shall open to the morning sun. Dawn breaks through to begin where time left off. And slumber in-between was comfortably soft. Awaken to praise Him, for I am here. Not to know the reason or grab hold of fear. I am here. Lord, let me speak first and always to You. Asking, praying, Lord what shall You have me do? This time was not gifted for reasons unknown. It was not gifted to keep to myself alone. Should I share these thoughts of God? Even though a stranger or friend might find me odd? No matter. God kept me here. I am here once again. Let me say this. It is He, my Father, who brings the morning kiss. From these very lips kissed by Him—I live. So allow me to give—give. I am here because He thought it good. Waste not one minute of the gift. "Write, write it down," He said. Oh Lord, I would, if You fill my mind with words, I surely would. For a moment my mind is still. Words, His Holy Words, I hear, "I AM." I believe this is the reason I am here…

I Am Here

Something moved me
Eyelids flutter to see
Thoughts not yet clear
God is here.

Night to light eclipse
Holy breath on my lips
A gift, another day
Father God, I pray.

Sweet glorious morn
Warmth now born
Eyes open to the sight
He speaks, "write."

He thought it good
So, write I would
A sigh, Oh dear
His Word, I hear.

"I am here" to write
Precious in His sight
Never, ever fear
But, draw near.

Simply imagine this
Feel the morning Kiss
To us a Son, the Lamb
Touched by: "I AM."

Jesus said to them,
"Most assuredly, I say to you, before Abraham was, I AM."
John 8:58 (NKJV)

47

I Am The Poet Story

I am not a defeatist or an elitist. I am the poet. I hold the pencil, but it is God who writes—and surely, I know it!

My last book, ***Hidden with Christ in God***, has a stunning cover, thanks to the expertise of graphic designer, Beth Basista, and contributing artist, Kathleen Denis.

I have heard it said that one can't judge a book by its cover! Nothing could be further from the truth. The only time you will buy a book, without preference to the cover, is if the author is well known and to your taste. So, does the cover really matter? It does, especially if your penmanship is not a household name. It is apparent that much detail has gone into the cover and it truly is an eye catcher, yet the book does not fly off the shelf. As a matter of fact, it may not even make it to the proverbial shelf! What then is the problem?

Surely, not the cover, as it is lovely. And God has a hand in the messages written between the cover. What then, is the problem? Is it the purchase price? No. it is reasonably, if not lowly, priced. Alright, the cover is exquisite, the writer is inspired by God, the price is cheap, and still the book does not fly off the shelf. Now the comment, "You can't sell a book by its cover," seems more appropriate. Now this brings me to the question: "What do people want to read?" You see, dear friends, when the cover is a spectacular preview for God, who is the main topic, then you must be prepared to be placed on the back shelf. But, to be fair, I cannot say that people do not want to read Christian books, because they do and they will. However, the average person, myself included, enjoys reading for entertainment and pleasure. I love romance, mystery, and action, which is what propels and sells, and has cornered the market for book sales.

I believe that it is indeed the cover that becomes the attraction. Beautifully done, yes! Professionally done, yes! A very nice looking book, yes! Hands caress, yes! Interested eyes detail the book and take a serious look, yes! Then, the realization comes from a potential reader---this is a Christian book. Hmmm. Hesitate, sadly yes. It sounds and really looks like a good read, maybe, but slowly the book goes back on the shelf for another time. The cover was the draw, the title, wait, wait, until I am in the mood for something spiritual. At this moment I just want to relax and enjoy a mindless adventure. Yes! Oh, but it was a nice cover!

This little note is for my dear friends who have supported me in this writing ministry and actually read a few of my books. I wish to share my thoughts with you all. I read devotionals every morning and I read just about every book that makes it to my library on the floor. For me, the cover draws, the title hooks, the author authenticates, and the price doesn't matter. Here is an example: I have many favorite poets that I have enjoyed over the years. One in particular is Eliza Cook. Most of you probably never heard of her. I bought a leather bound special edition, ***The Complete Poetical Works of Eliza Cook*** from the 1800's. I purchased this book from a curator in London and it is an antiquity in pristine condition. I paid $140.00, yes, that is correct, I paid $140.00 because... Allow me to digress back to the moment I opened the package.

I unwrapped a soft, tan yellowish leather-bound book. The pages were tipped with gold. This book was old. It had that peculiar smell of book, if you know what I mean. It is a collectable of all time, not necessarily because it is so old, so mint, and so expensive. No! It is important to me solely for this reason. It is Eliza Cook, one of the greatest Victorian poets of all time.

Now the book sits on my shelf, and mostly, I just look at it, as it is delicate and lovely. Sometimes, I very gently turn the pages for the sheer enjoyment of imagining myself being there in that time. Finally, I went online and bought an old durable hardcover of the same book so I could enjoy her works without concerning myself with damaging the book. Maybe I am a little weird, because I have a small library of books that are collectibles and these poets are mostly women, but for a few men who are husbands of these, and writers also, and all are friends with each other from the same era. These writers were the greatest, the most well known, but long-dead poets. Herein lies the fate of many poets, not these who enjoyed notoriety while living, but many poets will write God inspired works that will live on and on after they are long, long gone.

Well, I can live with that, or shall I say, die with that. Let's just say once again, the cover is awesome, the writer is God inspired, and the pencil scribbler is me. I envision this: someday a woman will reach for the shelf and hold in her hands a book. She will turn each page and find the perfect poem for her circumstance. She will wonder a little of the life of the poet. She will decide the book was worth the price and the cover is so, so nice. The writer is inspired by God, and the poet a bit odd and---quite dead. Yet, the words on the page yellowed with age have been reassuring that God is real, even after a hundred plus years. He speaks through those who are willing to write. In my vision my humble heart can see---the poet was me…

I Am The Poet

"The Poet's Dream"

Words plague a poet's mind
More truth than fiction said
If one should tarry in my book
When from me life has fled.

May the poet's grave be empty
My spirit with God to the skies
When time spans to antiquity
A stranger piqued by my demise.

The immensity of this possibility
That one might touch words thought
The poet cannot help but dream
An intellectual snared, then caught.

For what we write is soulful
It flows from our inner being
The words become infinitely timeless
When in the future, still seeing.

Yet, never once have I captured it
The dream is impossible to see
Till God in Heaven writes it
Then brings the words to me.

Long after I have left this world
And my soul reflects His face
A notebook labored in the night
But, no words to describe this place.

Still, the poet cannot help but dream
When a hundred years have passed
Another dreamer breathes her words
When the poet dreamed her last.

I Don't Know, You Know Story

"I wish I had a nickel for every time you said that," my Dad used to say. Even when I was a child the single most common statement I said was, "I don't know." Now, I have added two words to the mix. "I don't know, you know." Well, I wish I had a dollar for every time I have said this! But, the truth is, often times, when we utter this most dubious comment, we do know! You see it is never a matter of not knowing. We do know. It is a matter of faith, trust, and believing in God's Word. Once, as I was lamenting to my friend, she said "Oh poor me, the only friend I have is God." That stopped me cold in my "whine-fest." And certainly, she helped me establish one thing we do know. God is the only friend we have! I do know that the Father sent His only Son to die for me. I know this! Of course we all have friends and loved ones that we hold dear to our heart, but only God is able to give His all, His everything, because we are His offspring. *As some of your own poets have said, 'We are His offspring.'* Acts 17:28 (NIV).

Now here is something to ponder in the grandness of God. What I do know is far more important than what I don't know. I do know that His mercy endures forever. Psalm 106:1 (NKJV). So, what do you know? Do you know that your life is eternally His? Do you know that no matter what happens here, God is always near? Do you know that scripture tells us to *Delight yourself also in the LORD, And He shall give you the desires of your heart.* Psalm 37:4 (NKJV)? Do you know that the Word also has this promise: *For I the LORD thy God will hold thy right hand, saying unto thee, Fear not; I will help thee.* Isaiah 41:13 (KJV)? Do you know that His thoughts toward you are as numerous as the grains of sand? Do you know that He prays and intercedes for you in everything you do? Do you know that when you ask about His love, it's always "yes"? Do you know that He waits and longs to bless? Do you know that no one loves you more? This is what He died for! Do you know that He built a mansion just for you, and He waits for that appointed time when your life on earth is through? Do you know that there is nothing He won't do? He waits for you! There is no place He won't go, because He loves you so. Do you know?

One might say, "I don't know, you know." Some have suffered not. Some have felt neither loss nor heartache to bear. Life is full and rich and seemingly without a care. No prayers are unanswered. These ones are self-assured, and nothing breaks the spirit of the heart that has not endured. Again, one might say, "I don't know, I truly don't," and as long as you believe this, you won't. Oh, it is true, there is much that we can't know and it can surely bring us low. But, when you open up His Word to hear His song; a holy whisper that you have waited for so long. A poet writes words one might sing. "We are His offspring." This is paramount, this one thing! Wherever the Father would go, so shall we. For all eternity, we too shall go and "I don't know, you know" fades into belief, because at last: you know, you know…

So, now you know. Your only friend is God! You must trust in Him alone. For when the sun is shining bright, warmth comes after the coolness of night. Your eyes will wonder of the sight. The stars are invisible in the day. Think of God in that way. The stars are always there, even as the sun would shine, but only in the darkness of the night do they honor Him as they decorate the sky in a dazzling array. Invisible by day, yes, but what more can God say? It is true that there is much we can't know, and sometimes it can bring us low. If only we would look to the starry sky and see the vastness of the heavens that wait beyond for you and me. Someday, someday where you look, we will go. How wonderful! Now, you know…

How precious to me are your thoughts, God! How vast is the sum of them!
Were I to count them, they would outnumber the grains of sand—
when I awake, I am still with you.
Psalm 139:17-18 (NIV)

51

I Don't Know, You Know

Awakening to yet another day
Go through the motions and pray
A spirit feeling just a little low
Because- well, "I don't know."

Surrendering each morn, I sigh
God, I cannot help but wonder, "why?"
Mostly I believe that You care
Yet life is hard and so often unfair.

Lord, I long to see and to feel
Not questioning, for You are real
Please hold me, hold me tight
In the weighty sorrow of the fight.

Because- well, "I don't know."
But into the darkness I shall go
Now looking upward to the sky
From my lips I whisper, "Oh my."

Invisible are these gems by day
Father, what words can I say?
You created the stars so bright
That dazzle and decorate the night.

Though the stars are always there
I did not thank you in a prayer
Yet still to me You will sing
A holy voice speaks, "My offspring."

Father God this vision comes to me
The heavens there for all to see
For where you look, you shall go
How wonderful! Now, you know…

જીજ

The moon and the stars to rule by night, for His mercy endures forever.
Psalm 136:9 (NKJV)

I Just Want To Belong Story

I have a Facebook friend who often asks me to write prayerful poems for her prison ministry. Her name is Diane Missy, and this woman has an amazing heart for those who are incarcerated. It is not a ministry I am qualified for, yet over the years I have received requests from many woman and men who ask me to write for them. Diane is a bit more precise, because she asks for specific poems about specific people, and it is beyond me when this happens. The last request brought a soft moan from my lips. As I say to myself, "Are you kidding me?" What do I know about a mere child who is in this horrible situation and does not understand what God longs to give to her? Well, I put it aside because it was "beyond me." After a few days I expected to hear from Diane as she does not let me off the hook. I did not hear from Diane, but I surely did hear from God. I was laying on my bedroom floor, tormenting my body with exercises, when I sensed His words in my mind. "Get up off the floor and write the poem, Kathleen." And so, from my Holy Ghost writer, who always writes for me, I got up and wrote His words.

I Just Want To Belong

When I was just fourteen
What exactly did I know?
It was a little scary
Not knowing where I'd go.

I just want to belong
That can't be so odd
I was tough and maybe mad
Didn't care one bit about God.

When I was just fourteen
I thought I knew it all
Don't need you people preaching
Pick myself up when I fall.

I just want to belong
Come close and I get rough
No tears or crying for me
Back off on the spiritual stuff.

53

When I was just fourteen
This is what I didn't know
God was always by my side
Oh yeah, it's true, it's so.

I just want to belong
But life seemed pretty grim
So tired of being rough and tough
Started thinking about me and Him.

When I was just fourteen
Trouble always came my way
Now many years have passed me by
For on this most beautiful day.

I just want to belong
Fifty years I've lived since then
My age is an old sixty-four
I remember, oh I remember when.

When I was just fourteen
I longed for the pain to end
I remember the day I prayed
On that day God became my friend.

I just want to belong
And now at last, I surely do
Sweet girl, please hear my heart
As I speak God's love to you...

❧

Wherever you are, just know that I am praying for you
to know how much God loves you today,
and every single day, of your life.
Someday you will find yourself to be aged sixty-four,
and God will have carried you to that place.
I can't ask for more...

I Will

Photo Credit: Gloria Dingeldein, *Unstoppable.* ©

*I will not weep
Or stir my heart to woe
Nor open up the flood
That allows the tears to flow.*

*I will not grow faint
Or bear a soul bereft
Nor grieve for a moment
That my God has left.*

*I will not murmur
Or wallow in the night
Nor bemoan the circumstance
That has become my plight.*

*I will not lose hope
Or shudder in fear
Nor burden the thought
That God would leave me here.*

*I will not surrender
Or walk with the lost
Nor forget, no not ever
That Jesus paid the cost!*

*I will not despair
Or question His will
Nor worry the matter
That God loves me still.*

*I will not forget
Or neglect to pray
Nor hold back my praise
That God deserves today.*

*I will not be crushed
Or sorrow in my sleep
Nor fail to remember
That I am His to keep.*

*I will cry out in faith
I will wait and be still
I will trust in Him alone
My Lord, my God---I will…*

I Shall Not Be Idle Story

On January 22, 2011, *The Journal*, in Martinsburg, West Virginia wrote a wonderful piece about Mrs. Imogene Canby titled, "Area resident far from slowing down." This is a marvelous article and I will provide a short excerpt in order to give you an understanding of who God created in Imogene Canby. I see her as a mirror image of the God she served.

Mrs. Imogene Canby is a mother, college professor, substitute teacher, Sunday school teacher and real estate agent—she is semi-retired, but not slowing down. She is the mother of three grown children, Dr. Joni, Pamela and Calvin Jr. She said she has encouraged all of her children to pursue (their) wildest dreams and get a good education. "When I tell people about my wonderful children," Imogene said, "they say wow; all of your children are in helping professions and I tell them that my children learned what they lived. The Canbys work hard," she said, "and we try to help others. The most important part of my life is my relationship with God."

Mrs. Canby was born February19, 1931, and went home to be with the Lord on March 11, 2014. I never had the privilege of meeting this lovely woman in person, but I have been blessed with the friendship of her daughter, Dr. Joni Canby and I recently met her other daughter, Pamela. Now I can say, "I have met their mother." Dr. Joni and Pamela have walked the Godly life, as their mother shared and instructed them, to be all that they could be in Christ. Mrs. Imogene Canby was never "idle," not for a moment! She has left behind a legacy and a lifestyle outlined by God. Hard work and love for God has brought success to these who learned her lesson well. They are not idle. They learned what they lived because they learned from her. Dr. Joni and Pamela reflect a mirror image of a woman not idle, an extraordinary teacher, it seems; who taught her children to go for it and chase after their wildest dreams. And so I pay tribute and honor to Imogene Canby. I shall meet her someday, and on that day, I hope she will say these words to me, "You were not idle."

❧❧

She watches over the ways of her household,
And does not eat the bread of idleness.
Proverbs 31:27 (NJKV)

I Shall Not Be Idle

Though not one to be idle
It seems a burden to rest
This mind God has busied so
Then enormously, He blessed.

Though not one to be idle
Sometimes I wondered how
But God was my Counselor
And I shall not be idle now.

No, no, I shall not be idle
When all is said and done
Work is the essence of my soul
His peace lifts the rising sun.

Though not one to be idle
There were many seeds to sow
Knowledge breathed life in me
Having studied just to know.

Though not one to be idle
So I taught those I bore
To work hard, work hard!
Then work just a little more.

Though not one to be idle
Age does not diminish my zest
I am still on this journey
Maybe someday I will rest.

Still, I shall not be idle
When God calls my name
Oh, I shall not be idle!
For He taught me the same.

Dear ones, I shall not be idle
But if my heart should roam
Then I will run to Him, when
He comes to take me home.

In His Dreams Story

Yesterday, as I sat in my chair and watched my grandson play baseball, I thanked God for this beautiful young man. He is tall and graceful on the field. He is warm and affectionate off the field. His smile is affectionate and his words to me are sweet and will remain forever in my heart. He will be turning thirteen next month and I am grateful that this boy has tickled my ears with adoring words and reassurances that he loves the fact that I am his grandmother. This morning I praise my God who gave him good health. I praise God for all of my children and grandchildren. You see, sometimes we take for granted how truly blessed we are.

Today my heart aches for another beautiful young boy from our church. He is eleven years old and he loves to run and play. His smile is infectious and his hugs are sweet. His name is Patrick, and for reasons we cannot know, he has been diagnosed with Ewing's Sarcoma in the long bone of his arm. There will be three months of chemotherapy, surgery to remove the tumor, then three more months of chemotherapy. He will spend his summer, not on the baseball field, but tied to an IV pole and a barrage of doctors who will cure him of this dreadful disease called cancer. Our church family will rally around this child, even though we will not be able to see him because of the danger that we might compromise his immune system. So now the long journey will begin for a child who loves God, and a grandmother who will have the sole responsibility to take on the job of caring for and managing his life. I believe God will give her the strength to step up to the plate for Patrick.

Now begins the journey for a boy who has more courage in his little finger than I have in my entire body. There is no whining or complaining from him. He has said, "God will heal me." Once again I think back to my time with my grandson and my thoughts are simple as I read this Bible verse. *By my God I can leap over a wall.* Psalm 18:29 (NKJV). I expect Patrick to leap over the wall. I expect his grandmother will give him that leg up that can come only from her. It will not be simple. It will not be easy. It will not be quick, but Patrick will make the leap, because he knows God is on the other side waiting to catch him.

Will you please join our church at Upper Room Ministries in prayer for this child and the task that lies ahead for his grandmother to endure this trial to leap over the wall; to believe that God has covered it all? Even when pain seems to conquer, Father God will lift him up, now and always, in his dreams…

"These things I have spoken to you, that in Me you may have peace.

In the world you will have tribulation; but be of good cheer,

I have overcome the world."

John 16:33 (NKJV)

In His Dreams

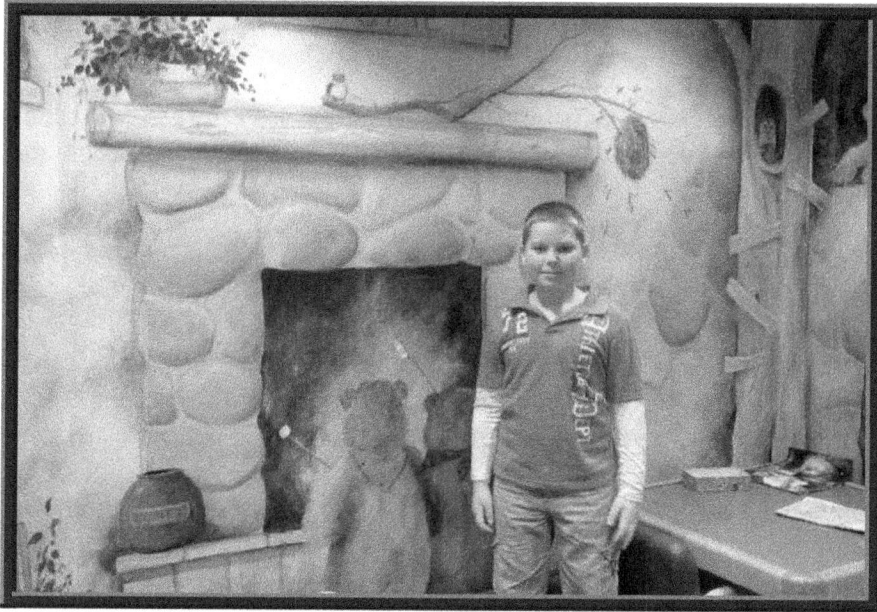

In his dreams, he runs
On legs that make him tall
He smiles, flies through the air
To leap over the wall.

In his dreams, he laughs
In absolute wonder of it all
Knowing God has lifted him up
To leap over the wall.

In his dreams, he sighs
Understanding that he will fall
Still, believing God will help him
To leap over the wall.

In his dreams, he prays
For God to hear his call
And courage comes to the child
To leap over the wall.

Lord, he has put his faith in You
Your Word can never be denied
This child will leap in victory
You catch him on the other side.

In his dreams, he rejoices
For no trial can befall
A boy who sings praise to you
As he stands before the wall.

This leap now a spiritual journey
The child may feel weary and small
But, by my God, by my God
He shall leap over the wall.

For there is no unanswered prayer
Even if pain conquers, it seems
The Father God will lift him up
Now and always, "in his dreams."

For by You I can run against a troop, By my God I can leap over a wall.
Psalm 18:29 (NKJV)

Interceded Story

Intercessory prayer is not for just a few. Intercessory prayer is for those who have come to that place of helplessness that may bring hopelessness, or surrender. I have been butting up against this place for some time now. You see, when it finally comes to this point, there is simply no place else to go. You have no wiggle room, so to speak, because your pleas have almost breached the Godhead. However, you shall not gain entrance until it is time; that is, until God calls you home. But, when life feels beyond human suffering, you may thrust yourself up against the Godhead. He is a breath away. His presence will hedge you in and intercede on your behalf. When God answers such a prayer, you better believe that you had a divine audience with your Father. In the Spirit realm, you were able to cleave to Him. He is willing, but you must travel that similar path that He traveled.

Oh, no one can ever actually experience what Christ suffered, but we can have a mere glimpse of what He did for us as we crawl our way through this preponderance or weightiness of life. Then, and only then, can we fully understand the trial. Its purpose is not to harm, but to draw us to Him. To cleave.

I have traveled this road, and painful as it may become, the end takes me to the entrance. I place my hand against the invisible wall of the Spiritual realm. He placed His hand against mine. He prays, He moans and groans to intercede. My heart has literally sobbed in ecstatic joy for His answer.

His answer was, YES! I have felt His love, a love not explainable, but attainable! Therefore, I have come to this conclusion, that those who have feared and suffered immeasurable pain have actually pressed so close to Him, as to cleave. Tears that fell vaporized into the Holy Spirit of God. My tears touched His, and He did intercede! So my precious friends, my Christmas prayer for all of you is to believe, pray and receive, but most of all cleave---cleave unto Him. For this I know, when I pressed close and pleaded; The Godhead heard---yes, yes---interceded...

༺༻

Wherefore he is able also to save them to the uttermost
that come unto God by him, seeing he ever liveth
to make intercession for them.
Hebrews 7:25 (KJV)

Interceded

Oh my Lord, I cried
Broken, broken
He cried, words
Yes, yes, spoken.

Oh my Lord, I cried
Surrendered, surrendered
He groaned, until
Yes, yes, tendered.

Oh my Lord, I cried
Breached, breached
He sighed, almost
Yes, yes, beseeched.

Oh my Lord, I cried
Touched, touched
He pressed, back
Yes, yes, clutched.

Oh my Lord, I cried
Cleaved, cleaved
He moaned, now
Yes, yes, received.

Oh my Lord, I cried
Pleaded, pleaded
The Godhead, heard
Yes, yes, interceded.

Photo credit: Kent Viklund

❧❧

Likewise the Spirit also helpeth our infirmities: for we know not
what we should pray for as we ought: but the Spirit itself maketh
intercession for us with groanings which cannot be uttered.
Romans 8:26 (KJV)

Let Time Stand Still

A Prayer for Chloe

At this very moment dearest Lord, I ask this of You; let time stand still. During the still, would You touch sweet Chloe, touch her soul, touch her heart, touch her body, at this precise moment? Should you miraculously heal every last piece of brokenness that has ravaged her body, let it be for such a time as this---let time stand still. Let pain and heartache depart from those who love her so and in this lull, heal this child. Because there comes a time, in time, when suffering can no longer be. And Lord, just between You and me, might this be that time? Oh Lord, the burden now waits for You to breathe the way. For on this very morn, You heard the families pray. No more, might we humbly say. Now in Your Holy presence, a collective sigh of those who love this child, stand side by side; we wept. Then close our eyes to wait for Your reply. Lord, bind up the wounds of this child who has become a most courageous saint. Let time stand still, for it can be only of God to fill, to overwhelm, to orchestrate the hour, the minute, the moment in which You, Father God, commit Your Word as so, and that at last, we know. Now then, You have heard the prayers of all. Breathe life from her to You, or You to her—whichever should occur; it shall be as planned. When the Master comes, time will stand. Still…

Chloe loved to sing, cheer, ride horses, play challenger softball, and eat a variety of foods, including, fried pickles! She loved her family, pets and her Savior, Jesus. She went home to be with the Lord on October 5, 2014.

Life Echoes Story

Life surely does echo from the moment we are born; life comes to us and reverberates back, over and over again. We can think of life echoes in regards to the things we say and do as fragile human beings. An example of life echoes is how often we inadvertently hurt each other, and most always, that hurt will at some point echo back to us. However, this is the way of man, and thank God, we who are in Christ, learn that the echoing is a teaching and humbling process, and inevitably it will lead to the end of life as we know it.

When we first open our eyes into this world of echoes at the hour of our birth, time begins to fly until the blessed day of rest when we close our eyes and leave behind this life. Life echoes from birth, to death, to Christ.

Shall it come? Oh, it absolutely will; when at last, time stands still. Life echoes to its close. In due time---oh Lord---He knows---life echoes...

≈≈≈

Life Echoes

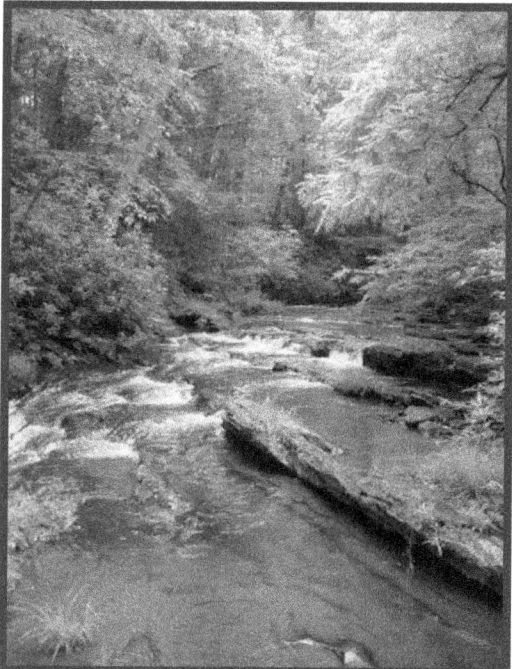

Photo credit: Gloria Dingeldein

Oh my, tears fall
In sorrow, I weep
Oh Lord, hold me
Shall it come, blessed sleep?

Oh why? Softly sigh
In prayer, a sweet repose
Oh Lord, when, when
Shall it come, life echoes?

Oh no, not yet!
In fear, I plead
Oh Lord, forgive me
Shall it come, I am freed.

Oh yes, it is He
In peace, God knows
Oh Lord, here I wait
Shall it come, life echoes?

Life Is Not What It Seems Story

If I have learned little in life, one thing I learned for sure; life is not what it seems. Sometimes, life appears to show favoritism to some, allowing them to pass through with little pain and great gain. Sometimes life comes hard and furious, even brutally insane, yet one thing remains the same. No one is exempt from what may come; even if life seems sweeter to some. If I have learned little in life, one thing I learned for sure; if I had not suffered, grieved, and fought to endure, I would have remained lost in my dreams, where life is not what it seems. Oh, if there had been a choice, I would have picked the easier life, but would I understand who God is and how He carried me through every moment of strife? If I have learned little in life, this one thing I learned; when at last we finally see, every heart shall bear His scar. Life may not be what it seems, but only God knows who we are…

❧❧

Life Is Not What It Seems

Life is not what it seems
But, had I suffered not
There would be no knowledge
Of the battle to be fought.

If life carried no burdens
Was always righteous and fair
Simplicity though often a comfort
In actuality is empty and bare.

Still there are those carefree
Who are oblivious to sorrow
Trouble does not seek them
As they dream into tomorrow.

The unexpected has not breeched
Nor crushed their worldly way
Believing they have earned the life
That warms each sunny day.

Oh Lord, hear my cry to You
For the heart that does not bleed
Not knowing the brutality of life
Or the blessing that comes with need.

Need may surely accompany pain
Though grief has avoided some
Even when life looks wonderful
Joy might not always come.

How can one know true joy
If we live it in our dreams
Without God to guide the heart
Life is not what it seems.

Life is not what it seems
Until we touch the deep
Whether bruised, or not, our hearts
Our hearts are His to keep.

Yet life is not what it seems
Until the Holy Spirit helps us see
Not who we are, but who God is
Hearts scarred with His, now free.

If and when the heart shall bleed
Fear not, for it bears His scar
Life may not be what it seems
But only God knows who we are.

❧

So God, who knows the heart,
acknowledged them by giving them the Holy Spirit,
just as He did to us,
Acts 15:8 (NKJV)

Lost To God Story

The times of being alone with myself have brought me to a place that I never knew existed. There have been many moments since Jim died that I felt completely lost. Every aspect of my life has been changed and rearranged. The past six months have been revealing in ways I couldn't imagine. Writing took a hiatus and reading took precedence. One day, with deep humility, I asked God to help me find my way; help me not just to read His Word, but to take it in and embrace God. But most of all, I asked Him to let me feel His presence inside me. I remember the surrender, not as a jaw dropping mind blowing experience, but a slight reverberation and an almost imperceptible tingling sensation that began in my fingertips and made its way through my body. I would have dispelled this feeling as a physiological aberration if not for my fervent request to feel His presence in my life. So, call me strange, or just plain odd, but from that particular day and every day since, I have been, "Lost to God." It is the sole reason why I can wake up and thank Him, even when disappointment seems to prevail, and I say seems to prevail, because all things that hurt, eventually goes away. Many days I have simply prayed for bedtime to come, just to reason with myself that I survived one more day without inflicting monumental harm on others. It would have been easy to step off the God path and visit the world I left behind fifteen years ago, but for this one word that screamed inside my head, "Danger!" I know if I stepped off the path for even a second, I would lose my way. There is so much in this world that pulls and entices us to look for peace in this extraordinary chaos we are now experiencing. It was my joy to be grounded with a man of God who was always, "Lost to God." Being lost can be the nightmare of your life if you line up on the perceived winning team and find yourself giddy with excitement over the most irrelevant things of life. To become lost in this world that has advanced to a place that leaves one relentlessly in pursuit of rewards that are fantastically meaningless has given me pause to think. I believe God has given me insight into a world I cannot enter, yet I will acknowledge with great trepidation that lifelong belief systems that once held great value, are being challenged, and sadly, placed in a hybrid faith mode.

Some have been caught up in an elusive and enchanting escape to a place filled with a myriad of mesmerizing make-believe. There was a time when I was mad at God for not gifting me with a brilliant mind. I felt cheated that my mind would not allow me to enter into the world of technological science. To write and publish a book was a most agonizing and exasperating experience for me due to my lack of ability and technical skills. But if you know me, then you know that God made it happen over and over. He placed people in my life to guide me and help me, but most of all He gave me the words and the message and the books. However, even with a lack of skills, I am easily drawn into fantasy in my own mind. I do not need any type of enchantment to find myself being led off the God path. Evil will always find the weakness, and cause me, or any of us, to make that ever so imperceptible step away from all that we know to be true. How about you? Well, I can tell you that I am sometimes lost and most assuredly odd, yet, found, found, found in the gift of awareness---that I am, "Lost to God."

Lost To God

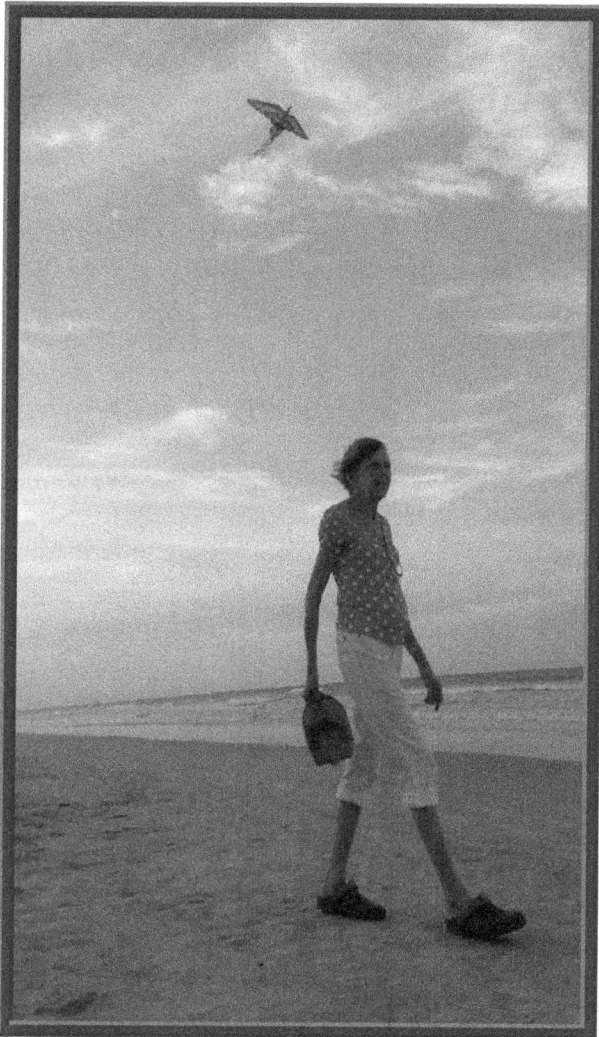

Photo credit: Kent Viklund

Can I wrap my mind around this?
Well, maybe, maybe I could
Deeply shaken by the thought
Not believing that I should.

A whole new world at my feet
Yet, stepping back in complete awe
Not real, not real, not real, but
Still, not sure what I saw.

Like a kite on a string, fly away?
Or surrender to the gentle tug
Down, down, down, feet on the ground
Feel the strength, warmth of His hug.

There is an invisible line, step ever
This place so enticing one must see
Some will visit, maybe stay too long
God, stay close, guard and protect me.

I was born to not know
These things that I cannot retrieve
The science is way beyond, beyond
What God allows me to perceive.

Not brilliant nor enticed to eliteness
I am truly and blessedly odd
But found in the gift of awareness
That I am, "Lost to God."

❧❧

Blessed be God, even the Father of our Lord Jesus Christ,
the Father of mercies, and the God of all comfort;
Who comforteth us in all our tribulation, that we may be able to comfort them which
are in any trouble, by the comfort wherewith we ourselves are comforted of God.
2 Corinthians 1:3-4 (KJV)

Measure Up To Righteousness Story

Once again, my mentor and friend, Stephanie White, has given me insight into God's Word.

Have you ever asked God to forgive your sins, even those you don't know that you committed? I know I have, and God is so tender-hearted in this matter. Sometimes we lose sight of the fact that Jesus died on the cross for all sin and we are free of every last remnant of that old self. Christ died so that old sinful self could become new in Him. Of course we continue to sin, but the difference now is that we are in Christ, and we will feel remorseful and then repent.

A person who is hidden with Christ in God becomes righteous. Some will say we are not righteous, but the Word of God is very clear on this. There are countless Scriptures that state categorically of the promises for the righteous who are in Christ, and nothing can ever keep us from Him.

So, as human beings, we cannot possibly measure-up, and fantastically, we do not need to measure-up! Jesus hung on the cross for us in perfect measure. He dragged the cross on a perfect line. He was born to us; a perfect sign. He died to bring righteousness to all. We cannot measure-up and most assuredly we will fall. Although we cannot walk the perfect line that Jesus did, still our hearts are tucked away in Christ and hidden. Oh, the promise of righteousness is ours to keep.

For the first gleam of dawn precludes the sun. His light shines on everyone. *But the path of the just is like the shining sun, That shines ever brighter unto the perfect day.* Proverbs 4:18 (NKJV). Now dear ones, what more can our Lord say? He has promised always to light the way! Righteousness was given freely to us when the Savior died---He filled our cup! The lesson: we can never measure-up! But, because of Him, we are perfect in righteousness! This morning, His Word has come to bless. For we are perfect, perfect in every way. Because of Him, I am righteous on this day. Recognition of the promise comes to me, knowing that we cannot measure-up. No, never! But the Christ in me is righteous, and that will stand forever! *When the whirlwind passes by, the wicked is no more, But the righteous has an everlasting foundation.* Proverbs 10:25 (NKJV).

Jesus Christ carried the cross in righteousness. He was battered and beaten, when on that bloody road He trod. Because of Him, we are hidden with Christ in God. *For you died, and your life is hidden with Christ in God.* Colossians 3:3 (NKJV).

Now a final thought to ponder. A plumb line is a tool to determine whether or not something is perfectly vertical or upright. It is absolute! The Word of God is the tool of perfection. Would you measure your life with this Tool called, "The Bible?"

Measure Up To Righteousness

Many times we try to make a move
But are we truly able to improve?
And is it anything we have done? No!
Righteousness comes from the Son!

The Christ who answered to the call
Brought righteousness to one and all
Because of Him the old passed away
His light shines down on this day.

Oh, the Savior God was crucified
Our sins were forgiven when He died
Not one of us could measure-up
But Jesus Christ has filled our cup.

Listen Christians! Have you heard?
All sinners are righteous in His Word
Remember the perfect path He trod
Now we are hidden in Christ with God.

For on this morning gleams the dawn
The righteousness of Christ shines on
We cannot measure-up, no never!
But God in us will live forever!

For he hath made him to be sin for us,
who knew no sin;
that we might be made the righteousness of God in him.

2 Corinthians 5:21 (KJV)

No One Knows Me, But He Story

Someone once said to me quite sorrowfully, "The only friend I have is God." This spoke to my heart, because if I were to have only one friend, I would surely want it to be, He. But I am delighted to say that God has blessed me over and over again with friends. However, this will not be a piece about friends. I shall call this piece, *No One Knows Me, But He.*

On Wednesday July 16, 2008, a dear friend wrote a lovely note to me regarding a book of poetry I gave to her along with a poem I wrote about her. I have saved the note, not because I love her, which I do, but because of the most encouraging words any person has ever said to me about writing poetry. Here are her exact words, "Thank you for blessing my life --- Yours is a powerful legacy, a very great ripple effect."

I have kept this note close to my heart over these past years, but this week the true meaning has come in a most profound way. I must confess that writers wish to be known for their writing. I have had many conversations with my friends who write, and we have prayed together about the outcome and the results of this gift that comes solely from God. Since my very first book in 2008, God has blessed me with four additional books and four devotionals co-authored with a precious friend. I smile when I read the note from my friend and her comment, "ripple effect" because, well, no one knows me, but He. I am not a giant in the literary field of poets. No. I am like a gentle breeze that bends a blade of grass or causes a leaf to turn over and over until it reaches its destiny. One tiny leaf can do much. Allow me to expound.

When we came home from Florida, our garage door would not stop going up and down. It was maddening and we decided it was time to call the expert, but Jim took one last look, and there was a tiny particle of a leaf sitting on the sensor. Oh, what a relief to find the leaf and remove it! This may not be the most eloquent explanation of power, but powerful it surely was! You see, dear friends, being referred to as a "ripple effect' was the most incredible compliment from a most incredible friend. No one knows me, but He, yet last week I received an email from Lancashire, England. A woman of noble birth has requested a poem to celebrate the life of her Mum who passed away recently. It is called, *Come and Sit with Me Awhile.* I wrote it for my Mom who has also gone to heaven. Of course I am always honored by these requests, and so I emailed the woman and her husband with my condolences in the passing of her mother. Here is her response. "Thank you Kathleen--Your work is universal." Oh my, now I understand "ripple effect" more than ever. No one knows me, but He, yet across the continent from England to Australia where a memorial service for a mother will be held, a poem will be published and read---So be it said, these words from my friend, "a very great ripple effect."

The Free Dictionary online defines "ripple effect" as "the repercussions of an event or situation experienced far beyond its immediate location." On April 9, 2013, the poem, *Come and Sit with Me Awhile* was read in Australia for a 96 year old Mum who went to be with the Lord. A powerful legacy indeed...

No One Knows Me, But He

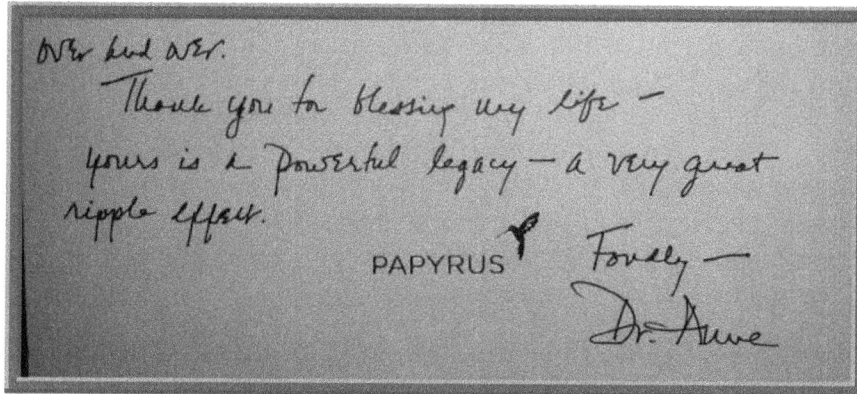

> over and over.
> Thank you for blessing my life —
> yours is a powerful legacy — a very great
> ripple effect.
>
> PAPYRUS
> Fondly —
> Dr. Anne

If you have no friend to call
If God is your friend, you have it all
But no one knows me, I bemoan
Yet, I will not leave the world unknown.

Time will pass and so shall I
A ripple? I wonder, with a sigh
So how goes it? The legacy
Will anyone remember me?

Now the message, a sweet request
Across the sea send my bequest
A ripple effect—a powerful legacy
But not, not to remember me.

Oh Lord, I humbly thank Thee
For words written mercifully
Remember, remember, remember
But not to remember me.

For no one knows me, but He
It is not mine, but His legacy
And one day I shall go
On a ripple my spirit may flow.

Powerful, yes and some may see
This legacy God gave to me
But, if not, so it will be
If no one knows me, but He.

Noontide Story

On Sunday, my dear friend and pastor's wife gave me a gift. She knows me well, as it was a very old book; titled *For Each New Day.* I thought it was quite fitting that it was a daily devotional. Not only was it in good condition, and lovely to look at, but this book was one hundred and thirteen years old. As I gently paged through this magnificent treasure, I noted that it was copyrighted in 1896 and it was dedicated to Mrs. Betsy Holton Moody, the mother of D. L. Moody. I must say, I really didn't read the dedication until this morning because I was so captured by the writers in this masterpiece. Of course, I went to the month of October to begin my reading, and I wish to share the October fifth writing by F.B. Meyer. Here are his words:

> Never be afraid of God unless you are sinning against Him; always believe that behind what seems difficult and mysterious there is a heart as true and tender as the heart of the sweetest, gentlest woman that ever pressed her child to her bosom. Nay; all the love in all women's hearts together, compared to the love of His heart is a glow-worms touch compared to the sun at noontide.

As Stephanie White and I are waiting for our upcoming Fall Devotional, I am completely convinced that God Himself choreographed this moment. Perhaps a sweet message about the love of mothers is culminating, but now I will say, nay. My mind cannot stop thinking about one word that holds me captive. I have never seen it in print and so the adventure to understand its meaning became a quest, a test and finally I was beyond blessed. The word was "noontide." According to the *Noah Webster's New International Dictionary of the English Language*, noontide means "The time of noon, Midday." Noon, can mean "Time of great power." And the sixth hour means "twelve noon in the Bible." This may not strike you as all that interesting, but I was compelled in my search for meaning and it was in the Holy Scriptures that I found time and again the significance of noontide. It is my heart's desire to share with you a poem that is completed by the Scriptures and this was rather intense in that I wrote the poem around the Scripture and the Scripture is the poem. I had an incredible day with a Holy God who is, and always will be, my Holy Ghost Writer! If only the darkness would have stayed at bay I would have researched the glow-worm. But, that will be for another day… Lastly, I wish to thank my precious friend, Diane Zawilinsky, for giving me this most valuable gift of words that has so inspired me to think deep and write in a very different fashion.

Noontide

The Holy Scripture bears witness to tell
Of the woman waiting at the well
Where the heat of the noontide would swell
Bring the merest glimpse of a fiery hell.

John 4:6 (NKJV) *"Now Jacob's well was there. Jesus therefore, being wearied from His journey, sat thus by the well. It was about the sixth hour."*

So, why has man refused to repent?
To the One who was heaven sent
This is the truth of what was meant
Not this vapor of life we were lent.

Jeremiah 20:16 (KJV) *"And let that man be as the cities where the LORD overthrew, and repented not: and let him hear the cry in the morning, and the shouting at noontide;"*

You shall not depart to an early grave
The womb protects, not meant to enslave
The noontide sun shines on the open cave
Christ stepped out for those He died to save.

Isaiah 38:10 (AMP) *"I said, in the noontide and tranquility of my days I must depart; I am to pass through the gates of Sheol (the place of the dead), deprived of the remainder of my years."*

Make ready for the noontide sun
In the thick of day scorches everyone
But hear the words of the only Son
Not My will, but Yours be done.

Luke 22:42 (NIV) *"Father, if you are willing, take this cup from me; yet not my will, but yours be done."*

Remembering a day of gloom so dour
God blocked the shining sun in stunning power
Yet, from His fate the Christ would not cower
He gave Himself completely to the noontide hour.

Luke23:44-45 (NIV) *"It was now about the sixth hour, and darkness overcame the whole land until the ninth hour, for the sun stopped shining."*

Yes, in oppressive times we are tried
Often searing, burning tears are cried
But, black as night was the day Christ died
On the cross in darkness, claimed noontide.

Amos 8:9 (NKJV) *" 'And it shall come to pass in that day,' says the Lord GOD, "That I will make the sun go down at noon, And I will darken the earth in broad daylight:' "*

Only He Story

I started writing this devotional over a week ago. It has been a long, hot, dry week and so has the writing of this piece. Finally, last night we had a drenching rain along with a volatile storm, but this morning as I read this piece for the last time I was drawn to my book shelf in search of the definition of a word I learned to hold in high esteem when I was only 20 years old. My Webster's was not the source this morning for a structured definition. I picked up my ***Obstetric Nursing*** textbook to clarify this word, "quickening." There are numerous references to this word in the Scripture, and we know it means life. ***And you hath He quickened, . . .*** Ephesians 2:1 (KJV). ***. . . He that raised up Christ from the dead shall also quicken your mortal bodies by His Spirit that dwelleth in you.*** Romans 8:11 (KJV).

My first encounter with the word was in my studies as a student nurse: "The early detection of fetal movement by the mother is commonly referred to as 'quickening,' or perception of life." (***Obstetric Nursing***, Fifth Edition, 1964). My second encounter was in the fourth month of pregnancy, when I actually felt the first flutter inside my body, the perception of life. The third encounter was in my fiftieth year, when the Holy Spirit of God came into my heart and quickened me, and I felt a new life come inside of me. It was He. My life, now quickened through His Word, and a Scripture I have often heard, ***If God is for us, who can be against us?*** Romans 8:31 (NKJV).

It is hot and dry on this day. Flowers have withered and drooped to a hardened ground. A few leaves have fallen down. The grass has turned from green to brown. The air is still and quiet. Not even a chipmunk is skittering around. A spider's web torn free, as a delicate strand dangles haphazardly. A tiny black ant marches onward in a soldier like way. It is hot and dry on this day. But, my heart is open to Him as I pray. This vision will not go away. If God is for me, who can be against me? No one is against me but my God; up close and personal, right next to, by my side, He is "Against me!" Sometimes I feel the heat when life becomes dry. It is time to reflect, and know that the cool breeze or soothing warmth so often may move away, maybe even cause me to veer into the void. Thank God, our Father is there, even when it seems that we are alone on this hot and dry day; step back a moment and lean into Him.

Oh, He is there; He is for me and He is against me. He is there. The vision comes before my eyes once more. So, I stoop down to my thirsty flowers and their sweet nectar drifts up to my nostrils. I touch the leaf that has fallen to the ground and feel the essence of the tree. I hear the sound of the bristling grass beneath my feet and notice it is the color of golden wheat. I revel in the peace of silence as the animals rest in their protected nest. My eyes seek the silky strand of the spider's web so intricately spun, now secretly hidden, not necessarily undone. Laboriously, the lone ant carries a heavy burden to the mound that houses these miniscule creatures of the ground. It surely is hot and dry on this day, but the vision of hope comes bursting through, come what may. A sigh brings the softest breeze, moves the thin blades of brownish grass; the leaf rolls and tumbles through the air as the spider's silky strand clings to an old lawn chair; beneath a spindly legged mistress hides there. The ant crawls into the earth to disappear.

Now the storm has come to bring a drenching rain, lightning flashes and thunder crashes to the ground. I sit in wonder of the sound, as life is exploding all around, yet the vision of hope remains the same. I whisper to myself His name, then I say, "If God is for me, who can be against me?" No one is against me, but He. Only He...

Only He

He is for me and against me
In His Word I have sought
This vision of His promises
What is it that He is not?

God is not unattainable to me
Remains constantly by my side
Up close and personal always
Still, so often He is denied.

He is for me and against me
Mesmerizing is this thought
Hedged in on all sides, forever
What is it that He is not?

God is not apart from me
He quickened my life to be
God is for me, who is against me?
The vision, the hope, Only He...

❧

What then shall we say to these things? If God is for us, who can be against us?
Romans 8:31 (NKJV)

The word, "against" seems to have opposing meaning in its own definition! Against can mean-- "to the proximity with (local, especially beyond or opposed to) or causal (on account of):—above, against, among, at, before, by, contrary to." (Strong's Hebrew and Greek Dictionaries #G3844).

Abraham believed in the later definitions and against hope, he believed in hope! I love this!

> *(As it is written, I have made thee a father of many nations,) before him whom he believed, even God, who quickeneth the dead, and calleth those things which be not as though they were. Who against hope believed in hope, that he might become the father of many nations, according to that which was spoken, So shall thy seed be.* **Romans 4:17-18 (KJV)**

God is with us, for us, beside us, against us, and often when I read the Scripture when it says the word "us" I place my name there (me) because God talks to each of us personally in His Word. Now---If God is for me, who can be against me? I am up close and personal to that word, hope, just as Abraham was. No one can be against me, but He (God).

Partake

Our God waits beyond the coming wake

Where faith swells beneath the bow, partake

Love endures for He will not forsake

Strength flows deep into your own heartache.

God waits

Faith swells

Love endures

Strength flows

Beyond the coming wake, partake.

∾ℛ∾

but rejoice to the extent that you partake of Christ's sufferings,
that when His glory is revealed, you may also be glad with exceeding joy.
1 Peter 4:13 (NKJV)

Peace Comes From Him Story

This morning, as I began my usual prayers and supplications, I experienced an epiphany! I have surrendered---but, I have surrendered far too many times. It seems, I keep retrieving the trials, as if I can resolve the problems. Think of it as taking out the garbage, then running out to the curb and bringing back the trash before it can be hauled away. Why is it that human beings can't get to the end of themselves? Surrender means to lay down, deny ourselves, our ego, and follow God. If God brought me to Himself, why would I continue to move away from His protection? Now hear this! You must get to the end of yourself before God can draw you to Himself. That is the true definition of surrender.

Once, Jim brought to me one lone flower. It was the only flower to bloom on my Rose of Sharon bush, yet it meant more to me than a whole bouquet of flowers. This one flower was enough to open my heart once more in surrender. The rose was a sweet and gentle reminder of God's promise. It only takes one flower to fill the air with the scent of life from the giver of life; not the fragrance of life, because this particular rose has no scent, but the essence of life pours out as our Lord says in Solomon 2:1-2 (NKJV).

I am the rose of Sharon,
And the lily of the valleys.
Like a lily among thorns,
So is my love among the daughters.

Our Lord gives another gift in time when peace has been ripped from the ground, dried in a deadly drought, burned to ashes, and swept away in a violent storm! Our Father God has an endless well of promises and gifts for us. I wish to thank Him for this beautiful, moving and life changing moment. Peace. Peace comes when we get to the end of ourselves; and then, only then, can the Father draw us to Himself!

I always believed that if there was a testimony from me it would be about the death of my brothers, my parents, and Jim's precious grandsons. I always thought that the grief and sorrow that came from death would be the testimony. But, this morning as I looked over this devotional that has sat for two weeks waiting to be acknowledged, a very different conclusion comes and takes me back thirty years or more. Has it really been thirty years that I have prayed for healing, for a pain that has controlled my life and held me captive, maybe even prevented me from becoming all that I longed to be? Twelve years ago I came very close to having a major and extremely drastic surgery. I had reached the end of tolerance. A friend, who is a surgeon, expressed that I would most likely be a candidate for this surgery. The quality of my life was so affected that I felt there was no alternative. Before we made the journey to Cleveland Clinic, Jim and I made a last minute decision to take a vacation to the Florida Keys. I had never been there before. It was there in Big Pine Key, in a tiny church, where the real surrender began. I became a born again Christian. A series of events brought us to Homestead, Florida, and unbelievably, we bought a little vacation home and a boat. And so, the adventure with God began. We returned home to Ohio to gather a few belongings. And yes, I cancelled the appointment and all thoughts of surgery.

Since that time in February of 2001, when we moved into our little house, I have prayed about this draining and most debilitating health condition, believing that God would heal me. Actually, I thought life would be easier, carefree, and so my Christian walk began in surrender. Well, I wish I could count how many times I surrendered only to take back the problem. And life; it certainly did not get easier! As a matter of fact, it went over the top with one devastating blow after another. My prayers became a morning ritual, that to this very day, is the most essential part of my life. Some might suggest that the "born again" experience has not brought the happiest of times for me and Jim. This is what I know: there is no way we could have survived the sorrow, but for the surrender. I believe God came at the most perfect time and held us close to His heart through these horrific tragedies. We have made so many friends, seen the beauty and majesty of the sea, we have lived through the best and worst of times because we let go and let God. More than once, I have expressed to my friends how amazing it would be to actually witness a miracle. You all know that my science-like mind would always look for the answer and possibly discard the miracle factor. Nothing short of a "Lazarus event" would satisfy my "why this" and "why that" mind! I will not go into written details, but will gladly share on an individual basis if you are interested, but I will tell you without reservation that not only have I seen a miracle; but God allowed me to be the miracle! When? When I finally got to the end of myself. Why? Because I surrendered completely. How? I simply stopped praying for healing and accepted what God had planned for me. What happened? A precious friend held my hand and prayed on my behalf for healing. Her faith was great. It happened on August 12, 2012, and since that night, I have been healed of my affliction. After that night and thirty years of prayer, tears, and finally surrender---I am healed! A miracle, unexplainable by science, and undeniably God! I got to the end of myself and God said, *You have seen what I did to the Egyptians, and how I bore you on eagles' wings and brought you to Myself.* Exodus 19:4 (NKJV). I would like to end this incredible devotional with one Scripture and one quote. *Then Jesus answered and said to her, "O woman, great is your faith! Let it be to you as you desire." And her daughter was healed from that very hour.* **Matthew 15:28 (NKJV)**

An excerpt from Henry Wadsworth Longfellow's poem, *Hymn for My Brother's Ordination* (published in *The Seaside and the Fireside* in 1850), convey it best:

> *Oh holy trust! O endless sense of rest!*
> *Like the beloved John*
> *To lay his head upon the Savior's breast,*
> *And thus to journey on.*

Thank you, Lord, for the rest of my life, however long it shall be; thank you for the moment in time and the peace You brought to me...

Peace Comes From Him

Oh, how I longed for peace
But not to ponder why
Or wonder if and when
As I brush a tear from my eye.

In this world of many wrongs
The answer seemed to flee
Prayer became quite meaningless
And there was no peace to see.

But who could really see peace?
When looking deep within
So completely full of oneself
Not realizing where I have been.

Then, God gives one lone flower
Now a beautiful day begins in awe
Surely not because of a vision
Nor what my eyes saw.

Peace came, it was an epiphany
The Rose of Sharon, from He
Surrendered and emptied my soul
Then allowed God to fill me.

"I brought you to myself," He said
But only when I reached my end
The Rose of Sharon rests in peace
For among the thorns we mend.

When at last we lay it all down
Even if life looks scary and grim
Peace comes, pulls you to Himself
Peace comes, peace comes from Him.

❧

I am the rose of Sharon,
And the lily of the valleys.
Like a lily among thorns,
Solomon 2:1-2a (NKJV)

Play The Miracle Story

This is a Grand Piano. I have never heard anything like the music that flows from this marvelous piano. I had the honor of meeting Linda last evening. She is a music teacher. And let me qualify by saying that is an understatement, because of the magnitude of her gift! She is a lovely soft spoken woman who said to me, "I have saved all my life to buy this piano." After I heard her play, I understood why a person would want this most incredible musical instrument. Allow me to express that this young lady belongs and fits perfectly with the Grand Piano. Now the most extraordinary part of my evening, was when she asked if I would like for her to play for me; there were no words to speak when the music stopped. I simply cried. The piano is indeed worth its weight in gold because of its magnificence; however the true value can be realized only when her fingers grace the keyboard. Her gift gave me a quiet peace. Now I long to share the joy of Linda Schramke Sproul and her musical gift of love with you when she plays the miracle…

Play The Miracle

I was weary on this night
My friend insisted that I meet
A piano teacher in our midst
She lives just down the street.

Oh, I was amazed by this woman
She sat before a piano Grand
Her fingers were long and elegant
Caressed a keyboard as God planned.

I heard the miracle softly flow
As I sat in the rocking chair
Her gift, beyond a writer's words
Felt the Holy Spirit fill the air.

A peace played inside my heart
A piano worth its weight in gold
But far more worthy and beautiful
Was the music that would unfold.

Play, play the music of love
That lifted my greatest sorrow
The sound from the soul of this woman
Shall carry me through tomorrow.

For in that moment I was there
In the Spirit of God above
Her music took me to that place
Play, play the miracle of love.

Linda Schramke Sproul

❧❧

Begin the music, strike the timbrel,

play the melodious harp and lyre.

Psalm 81:2 (NIV)

Respectfully Yours Story

A dear friend who has a prison ministry contacted me and asked me to write a poem about how women treat each other in prison. She explained that they speak to each other and act in ways that are lacking in reverence. Now I have dragged my feet on this particular writing because I now find myself lacking words for these women. I have given it much thought because I have never been involved in a prison ministry and feel very unqualified to write about their behavior. However, my friend has asked me several times to write, and now it is totally of God, as I do not want to sound condescending having no experience in this area of ministry. I prayed to God for the words that have eluded me. Because I have not been inside the walls of a prison, I felt incompetent to speak on this subject of those who are suffering and are incarcerated. I have looked deep for a common ground and then I saw myself. There have been many times when I have been less than respectful to my friends and yes, I have found myself distracted in church. But our God is so faithful. He gave me the poem when I surrendered myself to Him in prayer. For our words, our actions, and our thoughts must be reverent and respectful to God. Our bodies are holy to Him. Whenever God gives me a poem I always sign my name as, "His." I am respectfully, "His." So my precious ones in Christ, I hope that on this day you would pray, "Lord, I am respectfully Yours."

Respectfully Yours

Sometimes dreadful surroundings
Can steal away one's pride
Leaving behind anger and rage
Especially when freedoms are denied.

But if you focus on your freedom
That shall always rest within
No one can ever take it
You, you give it up in sin.

Your words that strike out
Then attack behind closed doors
Become a tool of vengeance
Respectfulness is no longer yours.

Steel doors may slam shut
But God remains with you
He knows your private heartache
And He longs to walk you through.

When prison walls encompass
Privileges once yours, now lost
Pray for strength and endure
Endure the penalty and pay the cost.

Trust God that all is not lost
Then learn to soften words spoken
Show regard for one another
Even when your heart is broken.

For darkness will surely come
Slamming shut those steel doors
These two words still belong to you
These words: "Respectfully Yours."

"Respectfully Yours," You choose
To walk fearless over life's horrors
Standing firm upon these words
Then become, "Respectfully Yours."

No one can steal your respect
But you can give it away
Should you speak in vileness
And then sadly forget to pray.

God the Father waits to hear
Your prayer as your heart soars
Tears fall when you cry to Him
Lord, I am "Respectfully Yours."

❧

Let the words of my mouth,
and the meditation of my heart,
be acceptable in thy sight,
O LORD, my strength, and my redeemer.
Psalm 19:14 (KJV)

See How He Loves Story

A few years ago, God allowed me to witness a most spectacular sight. A friend came to my cottage door in the Keys, around 11 pm, and said, "Come look at the sky with me." I guess I am easy, because I was ready for bed, but I pulled on my jeans and a sweat shirt and followed her to the dock. The night was inky black, but the sky was brilliant and dazzling as billions of stars twinkled and glittered their way to my stunned heart. It was a moment almost indescribable, yet a settling came over me as I rested in the absolute majesty of His creativity.

My eyes slowly drifted to the bay, and I was breathless with shock and wonder as the stars reflected off the water and gave the illusion of sparkling diamonds dancing just beneath the surface. The bay was still, and my friend spoke ever so softly to me, "I just wanted you to see this." I reached for my camera in hopes of capturing the scene as I tried to take in the hugeness of it all; it was so beyond anything I had ever seen. But, to my dismay, the photo was completely black. Why would God give me such an incredible moment and not allow me to capture it on film? I pondered this and now have come to the conclusion that He has blessed me time and again, and yet I have never seen His face. But, I believe that He is there even though I cannot see Him. On this night I felt His grandness and His presence above and below. There before me was absolute evidence of His mighty power to create, and so I will try to write and recreate the night.

Oh, the sight was beyond words, and I know with clarity that this magnificent view was going to occupy a place in my soul until I see His face. I expect God wanted to give me a solid, though intangible, gift. I shall carry this night seared in my mind forever as He has carved me in His mind forever. It surely was a supernatural exchange as the universe performed for me on the night of the quiet dance, where I could hear my own heart beat, and my breath expel, in a rhythmic sigh. I whispered to Him, "Oh my." For the stars of my Holy God spoke a silent language; a mere thought of who He is and what He has given on this very night.

I have no hard copy, no photo, no proof, only my words which seem sorely lacking in describing this divine array. So, Lord I am longing for another look if I may. Not because I don't believe, but because I do believe! The magnitude of power that shimmered above, then drifted upward from below, has captured my every thought. My dreams brought forth this thought: See how He loves. Just look unto the night—the sky exploded into life. I could have walked across the sea upon each glittering light to meet with thee. If You had asked me Lord, at that precise moment I would have stepped out in faith. There it is; the answer as to why, no photo. It is all about faith. I would have embraced each star to stand in that place where I believe You are. Magnificent, oh so magnificent was that starry night! Father God, might I have one more night? Bring to me this extraordinary sight and comfort me in your delight. And once again give me words to write. For on this glorious night, at last I see. See how He loves…

See How He Loves

There I stood in wonder
Stunned with absolute awe
The sky full of His glory
When billions of stars, I saw.

My eyes could not fathom this
It seemed a choreographed event
Stars dancing wildly in the sky
Have left me wordless and spent.

Still, there was more to come
As I looked down to the sea
Floating up like sparkling diamonds
The stars were reflected back to me.

I am mesmerized by this sight
In peaceful quiet I shall gaze
Then I thank God for this gift
He never ceases to amaze.

For if ever I had doubts
I felt them melt away
Tonight I look to a starry sky
And capture this divine array.

See how He loves, I say
As His Spirit washes over me
See how He loves, I say
From the heavens, it's Him I see.

Oh my, I see how He Loves!
A Holy illumination from above
In my mind at last I know
The stars, a revelation of His love...

☙❧

The heavens declare the glory of God;
And the firmament shows His handiwork.
Psalm 19:1 (NKJV)

See Through Story

This has been a long awaited and thought-out piece. I studied this most gifted playwright, only to acknowledge that even now, life remains much the same as it was in the 1600's, when William Shakespeare wrote *Hamlet*. There are two lines that have captivated me, and because of the many Christian elements in Shakespeare's plays, I chose to incorporate two of his most famous writings in this devotional.

Hamlet, Act 3, Scene 1: "To be, or not to be: that is the question." But the question for me is not, "to be, or not to be." The question for me is: how much of the Holy Spirit is in me, and far more importantly, how much does the Holy Spirit have of me? We know that when we ask Jesus into our heart, the Holy Spirit comes inside of us. We know this, but sometimes the struggle takes place when we cannot give ourselves completely to God. So, how much of me does the Holy Spirit have? That is the question. It is certainly not easy to see through the awesomeness of who we are in Christ, but way before my time, writers have seen through the eyes of the Holy Spirit and written deep thoughts in wonder and quite possibly, they knew. Here is a profound excerpt from Shakespeare's *Hamlet*, Act 5, Scene 2.

> Sir, in my heart there was a kind of fighting
> That would not let me sleep. Methought I lay
> Worse than the mutines in the bilboes. Rashly—
> And praised be rashness for it: let us know
> Our indiscretion sometimes serves us well
> When our deep plots do pall, and that should teach us
> There's a divinity that shapes our ends,
> Rough-hew them how we will—

Hamlet acknowledges that there are many things in life that we cannot control, but in the end, it is God who will prevail. Rough-hew means "unfinished," but thanks be to our Lord and Savior when He said, "It is finished." If we belong to Him, then we are complete and finished in Him. I wish to expound on the word "bilboes" as I had to look it up. It means "iron shackles." Now we sing this updated version of an old and beautiful hymn called "Amazing Grace" by Chris Tomlin. My favorite part: "My chains are gone I've been set free, my God, my Savior has ransomed me." These stunning literary works have comforted me and inspired me to write.

In 1603, when England was in such turmoil, Shakespeare's *Hamlet* spoke God's Name and Will. At this moment, I desire to see through. How about you? I desire to see through, crying out to my God to begin a work in me. It is not surprising that so often it follows what I call, "a direct hit." Life is at the very edge of our feet. It waits. We peer into the tunnel that is long and narrow, but the unknown calls. Divinity fills the air as we take that initial step of faith. A distant light guides the way. "Come to me child," we hear Him say. So we walk steadily toward the light, where God alone sees the end of it.

Oh, our incompleteness will surely endure the hit, as we surrender all we do, the Holy Spirit shapes our ends; "Rough-hew." This is most assuredly true; however with God, "Rough-hew" becomes brand new. Therefore, the question is not, "to be, or not to be," but how much does the Holy Spirit have of me? The answer comes at the tunnel's end, where the eyes of the Holy Spirit lend. In that moment at last, I knew---His eyes taught me to see; see through…

See Through

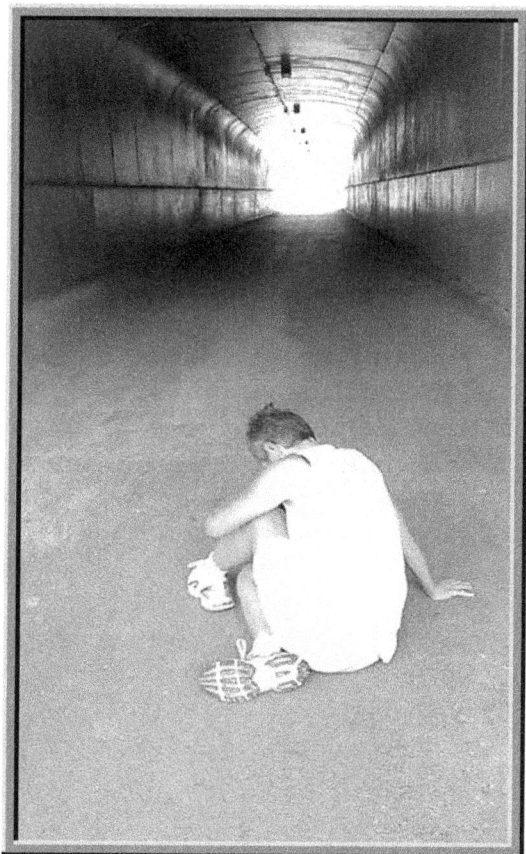

Oh, I have read and studied long
Embraced an old and cherished song
And when the Holy Spirit spoke to me
Still, still, I simply could not see.

But no one, No! Not even one
Could capture what Christ had done
The question: Did they hear the call?
For the Holy Spirit must have all.

The writers of old, deep in thought
Pondered in wonder the mystery sought
Philosophers from hundreds of years past
Wrote a tunnel vision of words to last.

I say, "Peer into the tunnel's light"
Then in His Divinity, write, write
Now walk in faith to the very end
See God's Words that you have penned.

For the Holy Spirit has called to me
To have, to have, and not to be
When I surrendered to Him, I knew
His eyes taught me to see; see through.

∼≈∽

. . . and to make all see what is the fellowship of the mystery,
which from the beginning of the ages has been
hidden in God who created all things through Jesus Christ;
Ephesians 3:9 (NKJV)

Seek Story

Here are my personal thoughts on prayer and healing. I believe God hears all our prayers and answers in His time, His way, and with our best interests at heart. I have had prayers answered many years after the asking, and I have had prayers answered quickly. I have had prayers answered exactly as requested, and others answered not exactly as asked, none the less, my prayers were answered. There are some I am still waiting for my Father God to answer. When I pray, I lay my petition at His feet, thankfully, and with praise, for Him who will answer. I never demand an answer from my Savior. I simply trust Him and wait. Because that is what Jesus did for me. He never demanded that I ask Him in. He never demanded or forced me to do anything. He waited in loving kindness, and so I have come to know that, according to Jeremiah 29:11 (NIV), He has plans for me, not to harm me, but to prosper me.

I do not wish to carry any more burdens as to how I pray, what I say, how much I believe---"Lord, help me in my unbelief!" It is a tremendous weight to place on a saint, who is a child of God, to suggest that one must do this, say this, pray a certain way, or state that God might not hear your prayer. For no one knows my heart better than He does. I thank my Counselor, my Prince of Peace, who longs for me to cast all my cares on Him. Sometimes I falter, sometimes I wonder, sometimes I question, and yes sometimes I worry, but my Lord never, ever leaves me. I do not believe God analyzes our heartfelt prayers for certain qualities, except for the condition of the heart. He is in our heart, so therefore He, and only He, knows the desire of the heart. I believe He loves our innocence in the request, our simplistic need to come to Him just as we are. I believe the Holy Spirit comes to us and intercedes when we simply do not know what to say or precisely how to pray. He comes because we are saved sinners. Thank you, Jesus, for our salvation. Our prayers should not be confusing, conflicting, fearful, demanding, and certainly not subject to specific rules. Prayers should be a spiritual communication between you and God without all the do's and don'ts or the threats of the won'ts. By this I mean, if you don't, He won't! I believe, if you pray, He will! He will answer regardless of the words you speak; all you need to do is seek.

❧

For I know the plans I have for you," declares the LORD, "plans to prosper you and not to harm you, plans to give you hope and a future.

Jeremiah 29:11 (NIV)

Seek

"Seek My face," says He
Lord, I ask, "Come to me"
In my dark despair
God says, "Cast your care."

"Seek My face," says He
Fall on bended knee
Call upon His Holy name
Feel no burden, nor blame.

"Seek My face," says He
To God I cry a plea
From my bed I praise
Down beside me, He lays.

"Seek My face," says He
My child I ask, "Come to me"
Do not worry of your prayer
You will find Me waiting there.

"Seek My face," says He
So a weary heart can see
It matters not how I speak
He will come if I will seek.

෴

Hear, O Lord, when I cry with my voice!
Have mercy upon me and answer me.
When You said, "Seek My face,"
My heart said to You,
"Your face, LORD, I will seek."
Psalm 27:7-8 (NKJV)

Simplicity Story

Years ago I would go running with a marvelous woman who was very bright. She was a dear friend who taught me from a perspective I could have never seen otherwise. One day, she told me as we ran, that I was simple. At first I was little insulted believing she was suggesting that I lacked intelligence. Now years later, I can smile at her near perfect description of my mind.

How does one of an average mind think deep? How does one of an average mind write deep? The answer lies in God's Word. This morning, in great awe, God revealed His willingness to show me, a most simplistic one, what He has done! I linger in Proverbs 8 as I step back in time.

I am a child, and my teacher stoops down to me. In my hand is a protractor and a compass. There is clumsiness as I draw my first arc of a circle. Years later, school become particularly trying for me, a dyslexic student, struggling to comprehend geometry. I remember those years and the complexity of math. Yet, even then, God was present in my life and He propelled me to the field of medicine, despite what I believed to be severe limitations. Certainly, there was not ever a hint of an analytical mind in me, but God would foresee. More than once, I questioned why the perseverance of these things caused me such anguish. Even a gentle and kind teacher would say, "Algebra is certainly not your forte." Still, I would not give up, even though everything was reversed and upside-down from my perspective. I continued to trouble my beleaguered mind to turn around, to grasp, and much to the utter amazement of my teachers, those mathematical courses I did pass. Oh, if only I could have known, for I questioned these matters of why. Why must I understand for example, "Pi" or any of these numerical wonders? Did I ever theorize in numerical terms the matter of "Pi" when I held the hand of a patient soon to die? No.

Now, it is forty years past those days, and God blessed me with a career in medicine. I was witness to sorrow, but joy too. Yet, my lack of brilliance had no quarrel with God, because He always shared, then instructed on what to do. I never needed the math, the chemistry, or physics that weighed me down. In all those years, the miracle was neither the knowledge acquired, nor the course and certificates that would bear my name. On this day they are but paper in a frame. But, I have found in His Word the reason for the preparation that carried me through life with a heart for the suffering--- unqualified and lacking genius, it's true; still, I have found the reason for the preparation!

Long ago, when the circle was drawn by a student's fearful hand, brings me to the here and now. Maybe the forthcoming of my advancing age might acknowledge wisdom, for I am on this most revealing page; the page in my Bible that tells me why, in simplistic ways, of the very first circle drawn by Him. To think I almost missed it, but He is faithful and my heart revels in this Epiphany! Here is the verse: ***When He prepared the heavens, I was there, When He drew a circle on the face of the deep,*** Proverbs 8:27 (NKJV). Can you imagine this moment? God drew the very first circle through the deep and the world was! I shall never look at a compass again in the same mundane way, but with the unfathomable mind of God, I pray. Lord, teach me, teach me as I am a most simple soul, the gifts that You would give to me if I should seek Your Word. A perfect treasure I would find. For this one written line has been defined—the incomprehensible boundaries of love and a Christ-like mind. The simplicity of the circle unfurled in that moment, when God created the world! In one line, blessed be, my eyes would see with sweet simplicity—God created me…

Simplicity

One verse, one line, an incredible find
That crept into a most simplistic mind
A memory, the struggles of a child
Until now, could not be reconciled.

Forgotten in embarrassment, I think
Yet God would connect me to a link
Then draw the circle with His sigh
That I query still, in wonder of "Pi."

In the depth, buried unconcerned
And in the heart remained, unlearned
Until a common mind could grasp
The enormity that the deep had cast.

But for this one verse now defined
God's perfection He witnesses in kind
Long before the hour of my birth
He drew the circle, created the earth.

Precious Father, I pray this measure
To always seek after the Treasure
Your Word freely given for all to keep
Stands firmly on the face of the deep.

This world we may not understand
Or comprehend what God has planned
But He has drawn love in my mind
A love not so deep, we cannot find.

It is a love that is so complete
Where the lines of the circle meet
Blessed be that these eyes could see
With sweet simplicity, God created me.

Yes, with such a sweet simplicity
God stooped down, gave me victory
Not to share an analytical mind. No!
Through my heart He writes His poetry…

❧

You gave me your shield of victory, and your right hand supports me; you stoop down to make me great.

Psalm 18:35 (NIV 1984)

Step Back Story

This piece is for me because of my inability to hold my tongue. Every so often, I scroll through my Facebook page. There before my eyes, words appear, inundated with rage. My human weakness wants to reply, but thankfully, I exit with a sigh. I do not pursue this aggravating and mean-spirited conversation. Purposefully, I just step back. Now, I say to you, "Just step back." Every day the page will somewhere continue to rage. It seems the world has set the stage for conflict. If you are one who simply must vent, then pray first that your comment will be heaven sent. But, hold your tongue if it quivers to attack. God will reward your gentleness and in His Word you shall never lack. So, when in doubt, I say, "Just step back."

Step Back

I say, "Just step back"
Step back from those who speak ill
They believe life has no good news
And live it as a bitter pill.

I say, "Just step back"
From words condemning, cruel
For there is much we can't know
Yet we see the words of the fool.

I say, "Just step back"
Align yourself with the only One
He knows the ways of the world
When all is said and done.

I say, "Just step back"
Don't encourage this evil word
Nor believe a mean-spirited comment
That your ears resisted, but heard.

I say, "Just step back"
For the critics can see no path
They are bound by anger and rage
Provoking even the Holy One's wrath.

I say, "Just step back"
It is wise to hold the tongue
Than to spew quibbling chicanery
That will always deliver the dung.

I say, "Just step back"
And wait for God to address
Our counselor, our Father in Heaven
Will dismiss this man-made mess.

I say, "Just step back"
With our Lord we can never lack
Read His Word only, then live it
Feel peace when you "Just step back."

꧁꧂

My lips will not speak wickedness,
Nor my tongue utter deceit.
Job 27:4 (NKJV)

Symphony Of Praise Story

Every day I ask God to give me a story. One Easter, poetic words were lacking. I told my friend that I had no Easter story. She laughed at me and asked me what I hear when I ride my bike. I had to think about that. Riding is about endurance for me. It is the time when I talk to God. Often asking the "why" questions. Yesterday was the Divine ride. My friend had encouraged me to listen; "listen to God's Symphony" is how she put it.

Symphony Of Praise

Riding, riding, riding
My day begins the race
Pushing harder to my goal
Relentless is my pace.

Riding, riding, riding
I stand to take the hill
A gentle breeze, His breath
My mind is quiet, still.

Riding, riding, riding
A cricket, a bumble bee
Flowers burst forth in bloom
These sounds bombarded me.

Riding, riding, riding
Leaves rustling on the ground
A dog barks in the distance
My thoughts become profound.

Riding, riding, riding
Baby ducklings waddle by
The mother hovers protectively
Little peeps make me sigh.

Riding, riding, riding
My hearing now acute
Having almost missed it, when
I turned my life on mute.

Riding, riding, riding
This cannot be denied
His Symphony plays on and on
I heard it and I cried.

Riding, riding, riding
Then the music from above
Down, down, reigning down
God's Symphony of love.

Riding, riding, riding
Oh, what perfect harmony
An eagle flaps her massive wings
When at last, I see.

Riding, riding, riding
Remembering for all of my days
Let everything that has breath
Sing to God a Symphony of Praise!

Take Heart Story

I wish to dedicate this writing to my Mom and all the Moms who are in Heaven. Oh sweet child of God, take heart. Wait for the Lord; He hears your plea. Look to the clouds and imagine the heavenly realm; for it is real! Heaven is not a fairy tale, but it is a promise from God that no one can steal! Believe, dear ones, reach out---Unimaginable joy is within your grasp. Envision the sight through the cloudy mist. Oh sweet child of God, take heart---Heaven surely does exist…

Take Heart

We must reach out beyond our grasp
To believe that the heavens exist
Envision the sight if one could see
The silhouette in a cloudy mist.

Oh sweet child of God, take heart
For the heavenly realm is real
And all that you may imagine
Is what God wants you to feel.

He comforts you with inexplicable joy
Then stands firmly within your grasp
He was never beyond your reach
When the hands of God, you clasp.

Oh sweet child of God, take heart
Your Father God longs to bring relief
Then wipe every tear from your eyes
Eyes that cry to Him with grief.

His promise is your truth and hope
When burdened and broken in despair
God holds your pleas to His heart
As He moans and groans His prayer.

Oh sweet child of God, take heart
Then reach out beyond your grasp
Feel His arms wrap around you
With a love that will forever last.

Now, for such a time as this
When crushing blows of life persist
Take heart, reach out and believe
In the mist, the heavens exist.

Oh sweet child of God, take heart
Live with hope, and not despair
His strength to you He will impart
God's boundless love is everywhere!

❧❧

I would have despaired unless I had believed that I would see
the goodness of the LORD In the land of the living.
Wait for the LORD;
Be strong and let your heart take courage;
Yes wait for the LORD.

Psalm 27: 13-14 (NASB)

The Foundation Story

My Dad was a veteran. He came home with the Bronze Star. There were stories from his brothers who also served with him. My Dad was a hero who did not speak of his bravery. Throughout my life, my Dad was always there. This little house that I live in has been touched by him in a thousand ways. We built the barn-shaped shed out back together. We did all of the digging and laying of the forms for my front porch and made the patio on the front of my house. My dad helped me plant all of the trees and flowers. Together, until the day he died, he prepared the ground and he planted my garden for me. Every Sunday, my Dad cooked fabulous meals for all of us. He loved to create in the kitchen. He was a self-taught chef, and his house was always filled with loving family. And of course, Grandma and Grandpa Bill came for dinner too. My Dad's little house was immaculate. His small parcel of land was dazzling with flowers and a rose and rock garden, which he took great pride in. He made a patio the entire length of his house that he laid in perfection brick by brick. You would be hard pressed to find one weed escaping the hand of my dad. I never knew anyone who worked harder than my Dad, and even more importantly, he shared all he had with others. He made sure that I got an education and instilled a love for family and a heart for those less fortunate than us. I never knew that we were relatively poor because my Dad was so rich in life. When my brothers died at the age of eight and four years old, I truly don't know what kept him going. In those days, marriages held tight. My Mom was his greatest comfort. When my Dad died at the young age of fifty-seven from a massive coronary, I lost all interest in this house. I had enjoyed my garden and my house. I sorely missed his touch.

It was not until ten years later, when Jim came into my life, that once again, I started to enjoy my house. Jim was much like my Dad. He fixed things. He planted trees and flowers, but most of all he cherished me. One day my Mom called and said that she wanted to replace the brick patio with grass. She asked Jim if he would pull up all the brick and plant grass for her. I can't even venture to say how many brick we pulled up, and incredibly, my sweet husband hauled all those bricks in the trunk of his car and brought every single one back to our home. We made trip after trip for Dad's brick. Jim had a plan. He put my Dad's brick in our back yard so I could enjoy the foundation and wonderful memories of a great man. My Father's patio was far more than brick. My Dad was a builder of many things. Everything he did had a plan and a purpose. My Jim was a builder too. The brick patio was the greatest gift he ever gave to me. I had part of my Dad, and now part of my Jim, to stand on. I watched two men in a labor of love, lay the foundation for the women they loved. When Jim died, I lost interest in my house again. I let the weeds grow over and neglected our once beautiful haven in our back yard. This past year, I felt myself slowly coming back to the joy of remembering that there were two extraordinary men in my life. I hired a builder for my porch and a landscaper for the enclosure. I told my landscaper why I loved my brick patio; therefore no deck would cover it. He worked for hours weeding and designing, and he called me outside to show me yet another gift from my Dad. It seems the neglect had moved and shifted the flower bed, but the landscaper discovered two more rows of brick that had been buried and lost from my sight. I was stunned by this gift. You may be saying, "So what's the big deal?" Well let me say that I saw my life renewed with the discovery of the hidden brick. I had unknowingly let the dirt cover over the gift. It did not cover the foundation, the rock, so to speak, but I did lose a little ground. I was stuck in the muck and the mire of the grieving process. God is patient, because He presented the gift at just the perfect time. My Father God stayed right by my side. The discovery of the brick was a turning point for me. My new porch and my patio are a source of joy and peacefulness now, because the men in my life who loved me beyond words are still with me. My Father God, my Father, and my Jim have brought to me this reminder of the exquisite nature of their labor of love. Yesterday, the first Hummingbird came to say hello. Hummingbirds were Jim's favorite bird, but that in itself is another story for another time. One day, someone else may stand on this porch and step down onto the brick. Its history is powerful in love, beauty, and the firm foundation that only God could give. Until My Father comes for me, I plan to share and embrace my time here and live my life in thankfulness for this moment, and each morning I awaken to my fate, lends one more day to pray and contemplate.

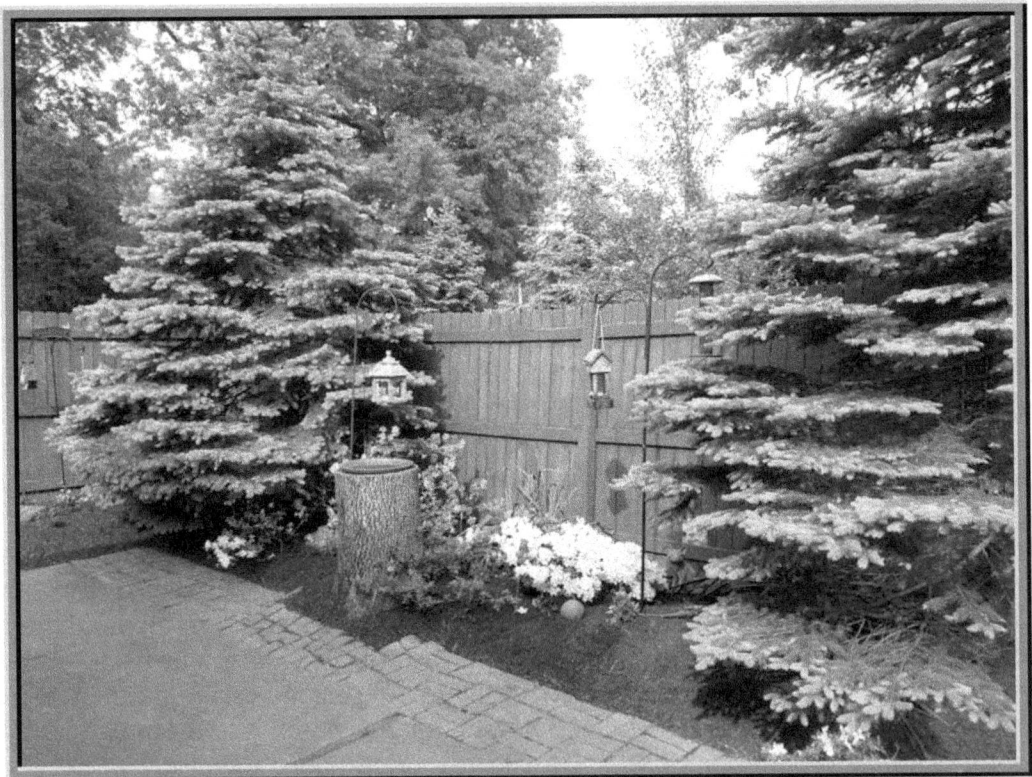

The Foundation

"I knew you before you were born," God said
The foundation was already planned
And a father was chosen for me
Along with this parcel of land.

My Father loved me beyond words
Side by side he taught me much
We planted and built together
And I miss his fatherly touch.

He left this world far too soon
But he gave all that he had
So I stand on the gift of his love
On the days my heart is sad.

My Father God sent another
And this man loved me too
He was generous and kind and caring
Taught me how to begin anew.

Now we planted and built together
Laid the brick that came from my Dad
When the labor of love was completed
My heart was no longer sad.

Through all of this God remained
In my joy I often sighed
But one day the sighing stopped
For the love of my life had died.

Yet my Father God was faithful
He waited patiently until this day
Pushed aside the dirt from my life
Where the treasured foundation would lay.

I am stunned by the sweet discovery
And grateful for this precious land
Praise God for His unfailing love
And the brick upon which I can stand.

Joy has come back in the memories
I shall live in the fullness of sensation
Because my Father God, My Father and my Jim
Built for me--- the gift of The Foundation.

The General Story

A few years ago, my husband Jim and I had the pleasure of meeting "The General." It was an easy meet for my husband because men just seem to talk a different language. The General was a very nice man, as was my husband. I can't say what they spoke about, but they were quite comfortable in their chairs and I thought to myself, how wonderful for my Jim to converse and enjoy this communication with a man of such high military rank.

Today, I was drawn back in time as I visualize these two lovely gentlemen in my mind. My precious husband has gone to be with the Lord, but once again I had the extraordinary pleasure of meeting, "The General." I was invited by my dear friend, Dr. Anne Stover, to fly out to California and visit with her parents, The General and Mrs. General. To say that I was in complete awe, is putting it mildly. Mrs. General, as I call her, or "Tutu," as her adorable grandchildren lovingly call her, was a marvelous hostess. She prepared elegant dinners that were fit for a king, while regaling us with fascinating stories and she sang lively songs, in German, no less. Her depiction of the military life was enlightening and educational. This was an intriguing chapter in my life to see and partake of what few civilians ever experience. The General was a kind and gentle soul. I felt with deep pride and emotion the honor of calling him, "Sir." It was a most appropriate title for this man. He surely was not in the least intimidating, yet never in my life have I ever felt that kind of respectfulness that was perfected in one tiny word, "Sir." If I were a "military brat," I would have saluted him!

But then, there was this brief moment in time as I was preparing to leave and I stooped down to give "The General" a hug good-bye and he ever so sweetly kissed me on my cheek. Instantly, I was transported to that place of uniqueness and eliteness. How many women can say, "I was kissed by a General?" It made me pause and think of a Scripture: *you stoop down to make me great.* Psalm 18:35b (NIV 1984). When I stooped down, "The General" made me great in that moment when he reached up his hands that would have saluted thousands of men and women led by him; he reached up those hands and cupped my face to give me a kiss. In that precious time, God allowed me to glimpse into this most amazing Smith family in their totality, with a vision of their success. The General and Mrs. General are servants; as well as their four children. Two sons have embraced the servanthood of the military with honor, fervor and dedication; their younger daughter is a physician of extraordinary skills, and the elder daughter is a humanitarian, business woman and speaker of extraordinary gifting. This family has touched more lives in more ways than anyone could possibly know. So here and now, let us salute the Smith family and honor the powerful legacy of Major General George Smith, who served under the leadership of God our Father, the One who stooped down and made them great. And so it is on this day, "The General" followed his very last command with dignity and grace; he marched onward to his glory, when God spoke, "George, Come up here."

The General

I called you, "The General"
Made you a leader of a mighty force
An enormous gift it was indeed
That would define in you the course.

Dear son, one day I will call again
A man who remained true to my name
For it is my Spirit that burns in you
That I, Your Father God shall claim.

I called you, "The General"
From a medaled chest to a shined boot
The blessing surely shall not end this day
From father to son honor comes, Salute!

Well done my servant; March onward
Hear a bugle sound as you draw near
I call you still, "The General"
Stand tall, Salute! George, Come up here…

The Last Half Hour Story

Some years ago, as I made my requests to God one morning, my heart was a little heavy. As I gazed outside my window in awe that God had blessed me with twelve wonderful years here in South Florida. It seemed that life was moving much faster than our bodies could maintain, and sadly, it was time to sell or rent our little house and simplify our life.

Jim and I had marveled at the majesty of the sea, as the ocean in all its glory brought the most exquisite moments to us. We had found peace and solace as we walked the sandy shores for all these years. We had spent countless hours fishing and exploring the world beneath the sea. We had felt the warmth of the sun, and our experience was beyond our wildest imagination. We have been extremely blessed by friends and our most amazing church family that has shared their passion for God with a generosity that knows no boundaries. Again, I want to express how thankful Jim and I were to have such an incredible life here. But, health issues and diminishing health care provisions had been the impetus for the decision to go home to Ohio after Easter.

I promise to take this lovely chapter in our lives and praise God for His gift that came to us because of all of our friends here that we have come to love. Thank you dear and precious friends, for the fellowship and sense of belonging to a family, especially during the holiday season, when we were far from home. I have prayed and asked God about our next adventure and the answer appears in one of my devotionals. ***Streams in the Desert*** expressed it this way: "The greatest challenge in receiving great things from God is holding on for the last half hour;" (March 5). The last half hour? Oh my, it has occurred to me that we are in the last half hour.

These past few weeks, I have been taking inventory of the possessions that we have collected over the years. There are many lovely pieces of furniture and artwork throughout this house. My very favorite is my antique white wicker desk. I am considering parting ways with the desk that holds memories of hundreds of poems and devotionals that God gave to me as I sat in stunned awe of Him at my desk. I must admit to my human carnality as I find it difficult to part with the many paintings of my dear friend Kathleen Denis. A few of her extraordinary works will surely make their way to Ohio with me.

Dear friends, it is not easy to let go of these sweet treasures and begin our journey into the last half hour. My Jim was feeling melancholy about leaving our little house behind and he had expressed to me that we may not come back the next year. Oh, not to worry, I fully expect to come back because God is so faithful. Allow me to expound.

Two weeks before we were to depart, our precious hummingbirds left as they always do, but it was a little early for them to leave. Jim and I always know when they leave as it is very close to the time when we leave. Everyday Jim would say, "Well, our little friends have left already." I told him maybe so, but asked him not to take the feeders down.

Just days before we left, the little one came and hovered outside my door. She chirped quite vigorously and brought her message of joy. The message was that there is much life to be lived in the last half hour. No one but God knows the amount of time, the adventure to be, or when the last half hour will call. Lord we wait in joyful hope for the last half hour, the last half hour shall be the best of all…

The Last Half Hour

Has time been passing me by?
The thought brings a heavy sigh
God, You have surely given me much
Now, I long for Your holy touch.

Another chapter comes to a close
What's next? Well, only God knows
His Spirit whispers, "There is more"
Before me stands an open door.

One more chapter written for me
Wait and trust, then wait and see
For a journey of trials and treasures
Intertwined with pain and pleasures.

Still, I thank you Lord for this life
Even when touched by pain and strife
Lord, You shall write the story's end
Through my heart, You are my friend.

When the final adventure comes to be
I will write the words in sweet ecstasy
The last half hour, I hear Your call
The last half hour, the best of all.

෴

For we have become partakers of Christ
if we hold the beginning of our confidence steadfast to the end,

Hebrews 3:14 (NKJV)

The Miracle Of Him Story

If you stutter and stammer at the possibility that God performs miracles still, and in this very day when people are so awestruck by themselves, it may be that God does indeed perform miracles, but He does not always allow us to fully comprehend the nature of His power. I am a hard core to win over. I must see it to believe, I must read it to know, and finally I must receive it to feel for myself the unbelievable, unfathomable gift that can come from prayer.

God is so sweet and tender towards me and my unbelief that asks Him to show me. So, He did, and these are my thoughts as a poet and lover of Christ. If one is willing, the very least God will do is to show you in His Word, the clarifying Scripture. Once again, He speaks to me of His works. Learning comes from reading. Here is another revelation of His power. Can you imagine that our God can turn back time in our favor? I would not have pondered this if I had not read it myself this very morning. Not only did God turn back time, but He actually heaped on more time. The story is the plight of Hezekiah. Please take your time and read Isaiah, chapters 37 and 38; especially if you are sick or suffering from a serious medical condition. Hezekiah was told quite frankly, to get his house in order.

"Thus says the LORD, 'Set your house in order, for you shall die and not live.'" Isaiah 38:1 b (NKJV). This is a paralyzing statement from God, not because the Lord said Hezekiah would die, because at some time we are all going to die. But, those last three words, "'and not live'" have truly caught my attention this morning. Here is what I believe because of my Savior, Jesus Christ. This body will surely die someday, but I will live eternally with my Father God in heaven. Death has lost its sting for those who are in Christ. I believe this, and it causes the burden of death to lift our hearts up to Him where life abounds! Now, getting back to Hezekiah; when he was given the death sentence; he did what? He prayed, and he wept, bitterly. What did God do? It is more than stunning! God turned back time, and incredibly, God added fifteen years to Hezekiah's life! *"Behold, I will bring the shadow on the sundial, which has gone down with the sun on the sundial of Ahaz, ten degrees backward." So, the sun returned ten degrees on the dial by which it had gone down. This is the writing of Hezekiah king of Judah, when he had been sick and had recovered from his sickness:* Isaiah 38:8-9 (NKJV).

Dear friends, I pray that you will be so intrigued, that you would read this story for yourself, but I want to reiterate this most amazing Scripture that has captivated me and has given me at least some enlightenment as to why I so love the sunset. I am drawn to it, and stilled by its heavenly display. No matter where I am, I look for it and take comfort in it, not knowing why, except that it simply moves me. This particular Scripture has brought meaning to the sunset and how God is so revealing. When I read this narrative, several phrases stood out to me: *"In the prime of my life . . . I am deprived of the remainder of my years.". . . "I shall observe man no more" . . . "My life span is gone," . . . "He cuts me off from the loom . . . "* Isaiah 38:10-12 (NKJV).

Here is the verse that literally turned the light on in my mind: *"From day until night You make an end of me."* Isaiah 38:12 b (NKJV). Well friends, there it is--- And this statement is repeated at the end of the next verse: *"I have considered until morning—Like a Lion, So He breaks all my bones; From day until night You make an end of me."* Isaiah 38:13 (NKJV). Allow me to take a deeper look at the enormity of this profound realization that includes this: *"O Lord, by these things men live; And in all these things is the life of my spirit; So You will restore me and make me live."* Isaiah 38:16 (NKJV).

Finally, the end of myself comes in this magnificently forgiving Scripture--*"But You have lovingly delivered my soul from the pit of corruption, For You have cast all my sins behind Your back."* Isaiah 38:17 b (NKJV). Can one possibly take this in without falling to their knees in thankfulness?

It is with absolute humility that I say, "Lord, thank you for bringing me to the very end of myself only to give me more time; thank you for loving me, but most of all thank you for the forgiveness of my sin. It is behind Your back. You cannot see it, and here I stand in mesmerizing awe of the setting sun." Here is the very reason why I have loved it so, spoken of it, photographed it, written of it, and reveled in it. It is the allegorical end of myself and the spiritually undeserving beginning of my life with my Father, my Savior, the Almighty God! For only He can stop the setting of the sun and bring back time until we succumb, until we surrender to that end, when the softening of light turns dim—dim—dim. Behind the immensity of the setting sun, reveals the miracle---the miracle of Him…

The Miracle Of Him

The end of light, certainly
Postures in the night, yet
The rising of the sun
A beginning of your end
Rise, rise for it is so
Another day, another day
Shall come and go
For the gift of time---pray
Even as the fading light
Shall surely turn to shadows
Dim---Dim---Dim
The miracle of life reveals
Look behind the setting sun
For the Miracle of Him…

The One Story

Last night I spoke on the phone to my dear friend and former pastor. He is caring for his wife who is afflicted with Alzheimer's disease. She is young and so is he, yet there is no complaining from this lovely man. He is filled with love and humility. God chose him to be the caregiver, the "one."

"Greater love has no one than this, than to lay down one's life for his friends. . . . I have called you friends,..." John 15:13-15 (NKJV).

This is the most unselfish act that makes "one" strive to be Christ-like. It is not hard to recognize what it means to be a hero. Just watch your TV and see the many thousands who have died for our freedom. Men and women have been dying for us in wars all over the world. For this I am thankful. Today, I wish to honor those who have laid down their life for another to honor God's Word. Now this particular Scripture, John 15:13, strikes me as not the giving of one's life to save another, but of living one's life to make another life livable. To lay down one's life means to surrender your life because another life is more important than your own.

I have seen this beautiful Christ-like gift on many occasions. It is the life of a caregiver; one who lays down their life, their heart, their thoughts, their needs, their hopes, and lives wholly and solely to give comfort to that one, their loved one. This depicts the truth of living this Scripture. The act of laying down one's life for a spouse, child, mother, father, brother, sister, and friend is the perfect walk with God in His Word, as it is written in John 15:13.

Because of medical conditions such as Alzheimer's, cancer, stroke, and the many emotional and physical disabilities, some have answered the call of caring for the one who is incapable of caring for himself. There is no greater love than this, to be willing to empty your life and fill it with another, as the single most unselfish act that will bring you close to God. Our God wrote this Scripture as a guideline for all Christians to acknowledge, and if need be, to live in His Word.

This past month, I have witnessed the beauty of God in His children. A husband cares for his wife who has Alzheimer's, a mother and father care for a son who is paralyzed, a grandmother cares for a grandson who has cancer, another grandmother cares for a granddaughter who has a brain disorder, a wife cares for a husband who has multiple health issues, a daughter cares for her parents who suffer from dementia, a son cares for his father who has a brain tumor, a grandson cares for his grandfather who has lung disease, a friend takes care of her friend who suffers from depression. And lastly, and most endearing to God's heart, a church takes care of a widow who is ill, yet she understands and comprehends the Scripture that calls upon each and every "one" of us to say, "I have called you friends."

Lord this is my prayer: "Allow me to lay aside the selfishness of my heart if ever my life is needed to attend to 'one' who is no longer able. Lord, if it be me who becomes the 'one' who is unable, give me strength and humility to accept my fate. And Lord, if it be sadly so that I should be alone, please do not tarry, but take me home." For the most painful life would not be the emotional or physical suffering that may carry us to our end; it is the loneliness and brokenness of not having that "one" who would hear the words of the Son, *Greater love has no one than this, than to lay down one's life for his friends.* John 15:13 (NKJV). So, are you called to be the "one?"

The One

We simply cannot grasp the loss
Until it becomes our painful cross
Whether we become the one
When at last all is said and done.

There is suffering and heartache
So humbling when we must take
Yet, if there would be but one
Who believes in God, the Son.

Rest and peace will surely come
Even when a body must succumb
Because God asks for us to care
Take the time to love and share.

And only time will truly tell
If we are the one, or the well
For the one who needs the friend
Might become you, in the end.

Life is hard and unpredictable
But God calls on the able
Yet sadly so many fail to give
In their own life they will live.

So hear the words the Savior sends
He says, "I have called you friends"
There is no greater love, cries the Son
When you are called to be the "one."

The Safety Of Home Story

Some time ago I wrote this devotional, but it sat as I waited for the Spirit of God to say "go with this one." So today, I am encouraged and shall go with this one, because my God is faithful, as always, to express to me quite patiently, and I might add, that He wishes for me to write what He gives to me.

As a reader and lover of books, I must share my thoughts this morning. Morning time will find me surrounded with books, especially devotionals. Devotionals are fabulously rich with words of hope and direction for living a life with God. Often there will be a divine revelation that inspires me to write and even think deeply. However, yesterday there was a need that no book could fulfill. I could not think, talk, read, or study. Every breath brought me to one place only: the safety of home, that which is His Word.

I was in my car coming from a doctor appointment with Jim and so I did not have my Bible, but because of this incredible world of communication, I did have the Word, all of it, in my phone. I read one verse after another until peace came. Here are my thoughts. We are blessed with the diversity and brilliance of others who love the Lord. Their work and ministry, though utterly inspiring, are simply a dramatic paraphrasing or highlighting of God's Word.

Each person has a unique and private relationship with God, and they write their heart and reflections concerning who they are in Christ. We surely can gather wisdom from these marvelously gifted writers, but I must acknowledge that sometimes I do not find myself on the same page with these precious ones, but ALWAYS I find myself on the same page with God when I am in His Book. For the Word of God will not confuse.

When I am in trouble, I run for the safety of His promises! There is absolutely no place like Home. Home is the written Word, God-breathed, His Word, His Book, His Haven, and His Sanctuary. The most important lesson was discovering that God wants all of me. He does not want me to turn to anyone, any teaching, any prophetic comments, or any other book that is not on the same page as He is. I can find Him in that most intimate private place in His Word, with Him alone.

As human beings, we struggle for answers until we recognize that the only answer is the safety of Home. And, that Home, is with God. In these times, there will be constant distractions and diversions for sure. The fancy condo looks good, but I say, "Stay Home." Do not leave the House of His Word. Turn the page to every room He has decorated just for you and me. I wish to thank Him for the comforting words He has so often written for me as I sat with Him in the absolute safety of Home. Gaius Plinius Secundas - Pliny the Elder (AD 23 – August 24, AD 79), is attributed with this profound quote that has stood the test of time, "Home is where the heart is." Yes, it most surely is, and as long as Jesus lives in me, I will never be alone. I will be sitting peacefully, in the safety of Home.

The Safety Of Home

Lord, help me sift through that which is not of You. Give me Your holy wisdom and direct my ways in everything that I do.

Lord, let me sift through that which is not of You. Separate this heart from anyone who would draw me away from the narrow gate I long to pass thru.

Lord, let me sift through that which is not of You. Hear my pleas and prayers in thankfulness as I lay them at your feet. Hedge me in and renew.

Lord, to You I pray in the Spirit, if my soul at times should roam, let me sift through that which is not of You, then abide in the safety of Home...

The Sculptor Story

For we are His workmanship, created in Christ Jesus for good works which God prepared beforehand that we should walk in them. **Ephesians 2:10 (NKJV)**

For we are God's masterpiece. He has created us anew in Christ Jesus, so we can do the good things He planned for us long ago. **Ephesians 2:10 (NLT)**

The Sculptor

He is the Sculptor, I the stone
Broken, jagged edges, I moan
Meticulously chiseled, polished to shine
Cast into the world to be a sign.
He is the Sculptor-

Yearn for this process of breaking
The stone a gem in the making
Now finished and complete
Stand before the King at His feet.
He is the Sculptor-

Go; with eyes that dazzle with love
The Father's hand perfects from above
Gather those unfinished, unhewn
For He is coming, coming soon.
He is the Sculptor-

Hold each one to your heart
As the process will surely start
Not one stone shall be left unturned
Their form at last discerned.
He is the Sculptor-

Oh, marvel at His masterpiece
His workmanship can never cease
The stone now priceless- Could it be?
The Creator recreated me!
He is the Sculptor-

Shine brilliant for the Lord
Cut and molded by His sword
When His work is finely done
Done-To glorify His Son.
He is the Sculptor-

The Shadow Of Turning- My Shadow Story

I am captivated by a Scripture, and my mind has been churning by these three words, "shadow of turning." *Every good gift and every perfect gift is from above, and cometh down from the Father of lights, with whom is no variableness, neither shadow of turning.* James 1:17 (KJV). Wow! These three words, "shadow of turning" are so poetically beautiful, and I believe the Scripture declares unequivocally that God will never turn away from those who stand in His light.

This was my initial thought when I read the words, *the Father of lights, with whom is no variableness, neither shadow of turning*. James 1:17b (KJV). I love the finality of a God who will stand firm, for He is the light of day with nary a thought of turning away. A spiritual shadow He shall cast. Morning, noon, and night, He remains unchanging and steadfast. So this is the here and now. In 2006, I started writing poetry, and I wrote a poem called, *My Shadow*. The poem was inspired by Psalm 91:1 *He who dwells in the secret place of the Most High shall abide under the shadow of the Almighty.* (NKJV). As a new Christian, I felt protected, safe and reassured that God was my shadow; that God was all around me. I knew that He was light and His shadow would follow me for all of eternity.

Now we are six years down the road, and another Scripture has provoked me to read again the poem. As I read it, I am in wonder; the sweet innocence of this writing because I trusted my Savior even though I did not have a studied mind in the Bible at that time.

God was a steady beacon of light. It was His hand that guided me to write. Of course, my curious mind could not allow me to pass up the opportunity to pull out my *Webster's New World College Dictionary*, that weighs ten pounds, at least! Oh, I could have googled the word "shadow" but there is something wonderful about the solidness of a book, and often I will go to the shelf, and pull out my dictionary to digest and study a word. We all know the meaning of the word "shadow." Here is the very first definition—"a definite area of shade cast upon a surface by a body intercepting the light rays" (Webster's, pg. 1231).

I could have stopped right there, but the poem that I wrote in 2006 did not feel aligned with that scientific definition. So my eyes continued to read the many definitions of the word, until finally, I found two perfect definitions that brought me to that secret place under the shadow of the Almighty. When I was a newborn Christian, God began to write through my heart, sending to me His perfect gift from above.

Here are two definitions that simplistically and spiritually define the word shadow: "11 a close or constant companion . . . 13 a protection or shelter" (Webster's pg. 1231). God is my shadow, even in the dark and loneliest of nights. He will follow me forever—He is the Father of lights.

The Shadow Of Turning: My Shadow

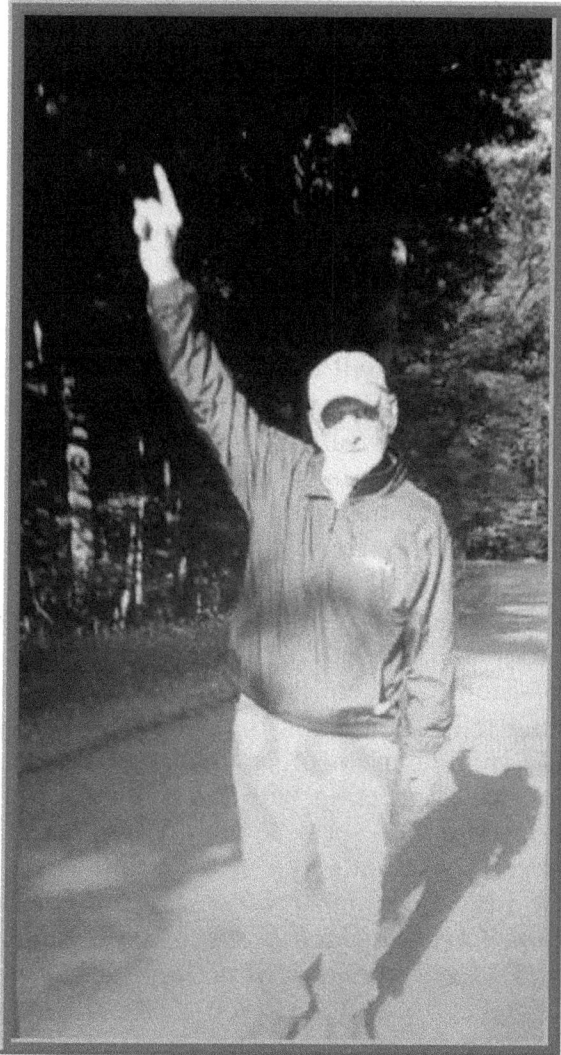

Lord, You are my shadow
As we walk side by side
Always present in my life
From You I cannot hide.

An all-encompassing love
Lifts me when I'm low
I am surrounded completely
By my God, my shadow.

But I cannot touch You
Yet, I feel You touch me
And I am comforted by this
Even though I cannot see.

For You are there beside me
When darkness takes the light
Protecting me, directing me
My shadow of the night.

On a dark and dreary day
His shadow lingers there
Just stop and close your eyes
Then see Him in a prayer.

Lord, You are my shadow
This I have come to know
You will follow me forever
No matter where I go.

∾

He who dwells in the secret place of the Most High
Shall abide under the shadow of the Almighty.
Psalm 91:1 (NKJV)

To Speak Or Not To Speak Story

This is not a Shakespearean moment, but as a woman of faith I am challenged in this area of my life. There will always be two choices in absolutely everything we do. Our first choice comes when the mind and spirit recognize that we can choose God---or not. Your choice of how you live your life, begins on the day you make this choice.

I waited fifty-one years to make this choice. It seems, I am a slow learner! Thankfully, God also waited. He waited for me. As I have grown older, life reset itself in a very peculiar manner. The choice changes the path, and the walk, reflects the talk. Yet more and more, the opportunity to talk, bears the surprising detours, in the walk.

Sometimes, one must simply stop talking! Be still. Look to the path before you. It is tortuous and winding, rugged and harsh, painful and arduous, progressively difficult, requiring the full attention of the senses. Do not speak. Just listen to God. Follow the footsteps of this wretched path He trod. Do not be shocked by what you hear, or stunned by the coldness of this world. Walk and speak not. He will whisper in your ear. I have made my choice. I shall quiet my voice. In this time of silence this windbag cannot sail, because I chose to still myself before my God who will prevail.

To speak, or not to speak, is not the question, but, it is the answer. Respectfully, it is my choice. Only in the silence can one seek, not anticipating one's own thoughts or words unique. Only in the silence, He will speak. For those who cannot refrain from their own voice—well they too made a choice; forfeiting the opportunity to hear the One who guards the tongue and embodies a holiness that charges us to take stock. So, this is my choice. What might yours be?

I believe God waits for us to pause---Stop the relentless pursuit of our personal cause. Let it be of Him before the stumbling fall, when down the path the fullness of one's talk subverts the ability to hear His call. Hold your voice! Do not speak at all.

Knowledge comes on the way down, to the meeting with the ground. Silence embraces the one who stopped vetting sound. Hear God speak to you. For all this time He has sought. Waited, waited, waited, until you spoke not…

Stand in the brook (ravine) where God says to Elijah, ***"Go away from here and turn eastward, and hide yourself by the brook Cherith, which is east of the Jordan. It shall be that you will drink of the brook, and I have commanded the ravens to provide for you there."*** 1 Kings 17:3-4 (NASB). Each and every soul who trusts in Him will stand in their own brook Cherith, and not witness a future dim.

To Speak Or Not To Speak

In the silence comes the gift to learn

He gives the power to the humble to discern

But those whose voice verbose, loud and shrill

He takes away the knowledge to instill

Not one word of boorishness so uncouth

Will ever speak the Word of God in truth

Listen, listen, listen to those with gentle poise

Turn off the voice of empty words and maddening noise

Stand in your Cherith with hope and resounding peace

In this time of drought the waters cease

Now stand for God who gave us all this choice

To speak or not to speak, I choose His voice.

❦

This you know, my beloved brethren.
But everyone must be quick to hear,
slow to speak and slow to anger;
James 1:19 (NASB)

Toil On High Story

I came across this devotional that I wrote several months ago. For some reason, I did not pursue this piece, but this morning as I read it over, it has merit and so now I will add it to my collection of words from God.

I have been feeling ill and stuck in my bed. Sometimes there is a dreadful anguish as I say to myself, "Why do I toil and who do I toil for?" The answer comes with the deepest sigh. I toil to pass it on. Now it feels like a selfish motive because it is a desire to ensure my immortality after I leave this world. So there is this expectation that my loved ones would remember me because of the personal acquisitions that I have left behind. So why do we toil? It is the desire of the self to be in control of the legacy?

The revelation here is that I long to have control of my life after my life has ended. There is no crime here in wanting to leave our property, money, and belongings to our loved ones, maybe self-centered briefly for the need to be recognized after the spirit has left; yet God is so merciful and understanding. He knows it will not matter when at last we see His face. But, there is that question again as to why we toil. Do I really want my children to whisper to my dead body, "Thanks, Mom?" Why must I always seek their approval even when death comes? Is this truly selfish? Well, I know that it is exactly what parents do. But, there are those who toil solely for themselves. They cannot help another, even their own family.

Sadly I have witnessed this covetousness, and thankfully, my family has been generous to a fault. Still, I have been guilty of this toiling, for I suspect we have been taught to toil in this way.

Here is the lesson learned, and how I felt when I went to the bank to close my Mom's account after she went to be with the Lord. I cried first, and then I wished I had known what was in this account long before she passed away. Oh, you can be sure that I whispered to her soul on many occasions, but never to thank her for the possessions. It was to thank her for my life. For if I had known the result of her toiling, I would have escorted her to the car dealership and made her buy a new car. I would have encouraged her to enjoy more trips with her friends. I would have insisted on every single item she balked at buying for herself to make that purchase. I wish I had known, because I did not want to have monetary gain and feel this enormous pain of not being able to share with her the legacy that caused her to toil on. Now I as a parent, I will also toil on, but for whom do I toil? Oh Lord, hear my cry! I pray to toil for You---I pray to toil on High . . .

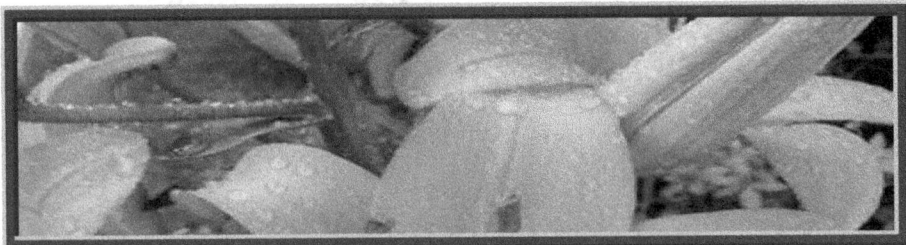

Toil On High

Toil on, toil on
It's what we are born to do
Gathering up our treasures, yet
None will leave with you.

Toil on, toil on
Some are abundantly blessed
Much more than ever needed
Still, selfish hearts possessed.

Toil on, toil on
A body quivers in a shudder
As sorrow grips the soul
That toils not for another.

Toil on, toil on
The wealthiest may fall
If one toils for himself
He might leave nothing at all.

Toil on, toil on
Foolish one soon to die
The Treasure that you toil for
Is the Savior on High.

Toil on, toil on
A tear will fall from His eye
If you should toil on and on
But fail to toil on High.

Toil on, toil on
If this is what is true
Let me toil my life away
But Lord, let it be for You…

❧❧

Consider the lilies, how they grow: they neither toil nor spin; and yet I say to you, even Solomon in all his glory was not arrayed like one of these.
Luke 12:27 (KJV)

113

Touch Story

One of the most notable slogans in history on communication was created for the AT&T Corporation. It was 1979, and long distance calling was encouraged around the world with these words, "Reach out and touch someone" ®. The original slogan was, "To communicate is the beginning of understanding. Reach out and touch someone." ® Here is the unknowing duplicity of that slogan. There would be no touching, but at least the audible voice of a loved one would be heard. The touching has become non-existent, thus rendering the computer-age techie as, "The Untouchables." I am not referring to the gangster movies of the 60's; I am merely acknowledging that we have given up our intimacy to the keyboard, the iPod, the iPhone etc. So, touch this screen and see me, is where we have come to be. One might say that we are still touching---just not each other.

Sometimes I cannot help but wonder if we have gone too far. Bill Clinton made an interesting comment. He said, "We should be in the place we're at." So, I ask you, "Where exactly are we?" "We should be in the place we're at," but many of us are not. Mr. Clinton revealed that he was ten years old when the family got their first TV. This is also true for me. That made storytelling and family interaction a common place occurrence in our home. Modern technology in communication, though unparalleled, has stopped us from being in the place we're at. I may speak to you, you, and you, but not reach out and touch your hand. Yes, touching the hand may be a simple gesture, yet there is warmth and intimacy in the act. It is hard to feel warmth in a text or email and that is a fact. The hand I wish to touch is most likely running its fingers rapidly over a keyboard, or tapping a screen somewhere where we're not. Oh, I am surely not against technology, and these most amazing advancements in connectivity. I am concerned about the solitude and isolation of the human being who would rather text a person in the same house within audible range instead of walking a few steps to speak eye to eye. And, at the very least, place your phone to your ear and actually call your friend or loved one and give them the gift of your voice. That act was the true meaning in 1979---to "reach out and touch someone!" ® Oh yes, "we should be in the place we're at" every now and then. We should have that kind of regard for each other. Are we too busy to even have the desire for the act of touch? Have we forgotten that it once meant so much?

In all fairness, I shall admit that this concern is one that will enlighten only those of substantial age, who find the new world of communication difficult and hard to decipher. For there is a mind-blowing wonder of the intricacies of communication in such a time as this. Still, I ponder the price to be paid regarding the forward movement of a technology that will replace the act of touching. Allow me to use an obscure and subtle event that will occur most likely in my lifetime, God willing. In Nepal there is a seventy-five year old woman whose name is Gyan Maiyi Sen. She speaks a language called, Kusunda. She is the only living person that knows the language, and when she dies, Kusunda will become extinct. The reason it will become extinct is because the language is no longer taught to children. This is just merely an example of how words and communication skills can become obsolete. Well, this moment in time and place will certainly not cause a stir in our world, yet I believe it will be a stone removed from the foundation of communication, and be insidiously detrimental to the extinction of the human race, to communicate face to face. Our children are the reason why communication will move forward for hundreds of years. When we stop teaching, we stop reaching "We should be in the place we're at." There are no words that speak more succinctly than that, and on the near horizon, is the imminent loss of human touch. To me, this is an anathema to the future of the world, as such...

Touch

There is nothing quite like touch
For the intimacy means so much
Now, technology has stolen this
And the warmth of touch, I miss.

Reach out and touch someone
Then tap, tap, tap, it's done
When a busy mind moves on
A person once there, now gone.

We should be in the place we're at
But no more is the chance of that
Connectivity though incredibly designed
Rearranged humanality once defined.

No more contact eye to eye
No more embracing with a sigh
We are not in the place we're at
When we choose to begin the chat.

Oh, I am so very sorry for this
And the softness of the kiss
To hear your voice, see your smile
Sit beside you and visit awhile.

Get with the times, they may say
The recorded voice has stripped away
But to my heart, I shall clutch
Your voice, eyes, hand and touch.

So tap away if you will
Yet I remain faithful still
Never to change and that is that!
In the place where I am at...

Treasures Of The Heart Story

In 2013, when we were staying in the Keys, I walked down to the bay to pray and thank God for the time we had shared on this property. Another couple was staying in the main house with their little boy. The boy was bubbling with excitement, and he seemed to be on a constant quest and adventure to find treasures. He had collected a variety of sea shells and coconuts. It was a delight to watch him as he appreciates the joy of life in the simplistic way of a child. Some of you know that Jim had a serious nose bleed during that time, and had a compression rocket placed in his nose. It was very painful, and even though Jim had had a difficult time, he wanted to watch the sunset, so we walked to the bay and sat in the love seat to see our 75th sunset.

Of course, little Luke was in search of sea shells, and every few minutes he would come in awe to each of us and display his treasures cupped in his precious hands. His joy and exuberance brought a smile to our faces. When the sunset faded, we were getting ready to go back to our cottage, but this tender hearted child came up to Jim and sat in the chair beside him. Luke asked Jim what happened to his nose and Jim told him of his hospital trip. Then much to Jim's amazement, the child opened up his hands and said, "I got all these shells for you." Luke poured his treasure gently into Jim's hands. ,Jim was speechless and his eyes welled up with tears.

When we got back to the cottage, Jim asked me for an envelope to put the shells in and I wrote "From Luke" and the date, "3-17-2013," on the envelope. As I watched my husband limp slowly to the closet and place the envelope in his suitcase for safe keeping, I understood that God is continually showing us what it means to love. This little boy is obviously in a loving home and being raised in a loving way. I saw his father hold him close and give him a kiss on the top of his head. The treasures of life are where the heart is, and I thank God for being "His" and for this lesson from a little boy who gave all that he had in one simple act. Now I pray, for this is what love requires of me; if as this little child we all could be...

Treasures Of The Heart

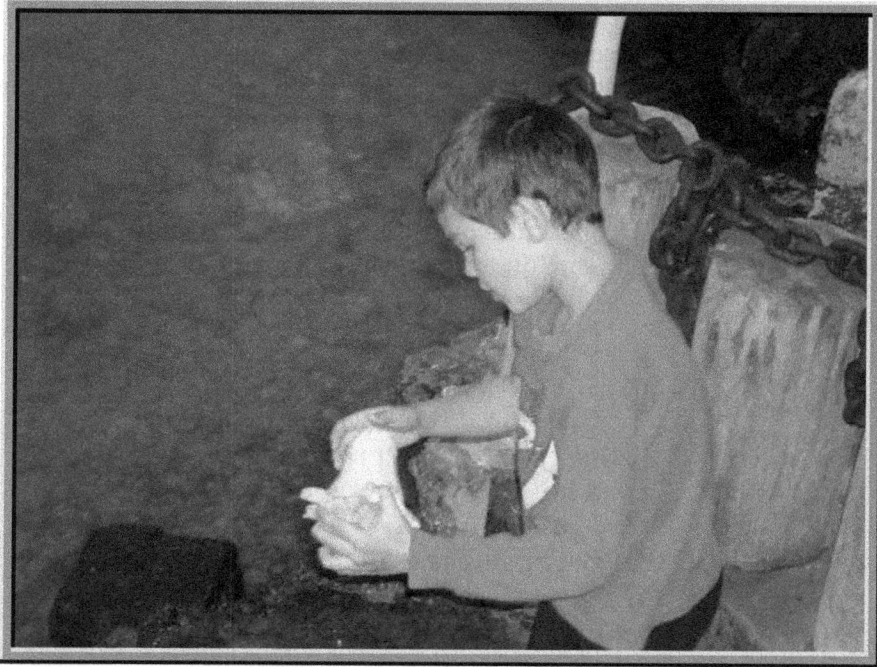

What does love require of me?
Through my tears my heart will see
Knowing where my treasure is
Like this little boy, I am "His."

For every lesson I have learned
None like this have been discerned
As this boy we all can be
Giving our all can set us free.

A boy named Luke held in his hand
Precious shells and glistening sand
With his smile, love reigned that day
When treasured shells, he gave away.

The father pulled Luke to his heart
This man and son shall never part
No matter where the son will go
He'll leave behind his heart also.

Luke 12:34 speaks of this child
Who possessed a heart meek and mild
And a father who would love him so
From the father's heart, his child would know.

That love requires we give our all
In that moment hear God's call
Through my tears, my heart would see
If as this child, we all could be…

❧

For where your treasure is, there your heart will be also.
Luke 12:34 (NKJV)

We Love You Too Story

In some ways, it seems like just last night that Jim and I spent a lovely evening with Ron and Tina Hudack. We sat on the patio in their backyard and witnessed the incredible display of God's creations. It was as if God said, "I love you so," then He began the show. Hummingbirds flew magically by, and one by one they made us cry. We could not help but wonder at the sight. They were an absolute delight. The sun shone down on colors bright, until a dark cloud smothered the light. Still, they came, two, three, then four, and zip, zip, zip, up they'd soar. We were so thankful for this time, to renew in the joy of these tiny ones, and everything that God would do. But most of all, let us never forget to say, "We love You too…"

We Love You Too

God says, "I love you so
And I will never let you go."
Look up! He presents the show.

We saw the sweetest hummingbird
Flying backwards, seemed absurd
Then its precious chirps were heard.

Exquisite and remarkable it was
But more incredible what it does
How so, precious one? Because.

Because God designed and created
Now every second that we waited
Watched in awe and anticipated.

In awe of this adorable little one
And the amazing work God has done
Red and green wings fan the sun.

Until a dark cloud covers the sky
Still feathers zip, zip frantically by
Unbelievable as we all sigh.

To witness this wonder from on high
Two, three, then four together fly
Bringing a tear to every eye.

A magical moment has occurred
Lord, thank you for this tiny bird
Oh, how we marvel in Your Word.

For every gift that comes from You
These miracles of life renew
But most of all, we love You too…

৵৶

"Look at the birds of the air, for they neither sow nor reap nor gather into the barns;
yet your heavenly Father feeds them. Are you not of my value than they?"
Matthew 6:26 (NKJV)

What's It All About Story

Sometimes Christians take a little flack over saying, "The Sinner's Prayer." It is quite true that this prayer is not actually written in the Scriptures. So, maybe sinners have created a dialogue in a prayer to Jesus, and I find this prayer to be an intimate way to commune with God. It is not only a longing to belong to Him, but also there is a longing for repentance. And this repentance is expressed publically to our Lord and Savior as a heart and soul is laid bare. The prayer is just that; a prayer to Christ asking Him to come into one's heart. Though the prayer is not in the Bible, there is so much of our written communication with God that has become a prayer, a lesson, or a song. All of this is a holy communication, and certainly not wrong! Amazingly, it is written in the Scripture several times, and you can surely speak it, teach it, and live it as it is written. For in the sinner's prayer, created by Christians, we are simply asking Christ to come in. Now read, 1 Corinthians 1:30-31, ***But of Him you are in Christ Jesus, who became for us wisdom from God--and righteousness and sanctification and redemption--that, as it is written, "He who glories, let him glory in the LORD."*** (NKJV).

My heart is overwhelmed by this fact: ***"But of Him you are in Christ!"*** I am in Christ! When I finally comprehend this Scriptural written word, it takes me to my knees.

Imagine Him surrounding you on all sides! You are in Him! Now here is the most extraordinary gift of all, and the Scripture states it quite clearly; Christ is in me! According to Colossians 1:27, ***To them God willed to make known what are the riches of the glory of this mystery among the Gentiles: which is Christ in you, the hope of glory.*** (NKJV). Now, I am in His unfathom**able**, unimagin**able**, inconceiv**able**, and unbeliev**able** heart! Notice that each adjective ends in "**able**." And this is so apropos, for He is able and I am not. He is able, and these words of hope I shout! You are in Him and He is in you! That's what the Christian life is all about…

What's It All About

Some are a little conflicted
About saying the sinner's prayer
No worries for God is smiling
He loves the heart laid bare.

But will Jesus walk into a heart
Just because of a simple prayer?
Again I say no worries dear ones
I believe God is already there.

No one knows your heart like God
If with Him you truly long to be
Christ gives the invitation to all
"Come live in Me," says He.

"But of Him you are in Christ Jesus
Who became for us wisdom from God"*
Though not a prayer, but a walk
Down the rugged path Jesus trod.

You are in Him and He in you!
Words of hope and glory, I shout!
For He is able and I am not!
That's what the Christian life's all about.

❧❧

For God so loved the world
that He gave
His only begotten Son,
that whoever believes in Him
should not perish
but have everlasting life.
John 3:16 (NKJV)

* I Corinthians 1:30 (NKJV)

Whosoever Story

And the Spirit and the bride say, Come. And let him that heareth say, Come. And let him that is athirst come. And whosoever will, let him take the water of life freely. Revelation 22:17 (KJV).

Here is the invitation to become His! We are invited to "Come" to Christ. Absolutely everyone is invited! Whosoever desires, can accept. Who---this could be you. Soever---this is forever! I thirst for Him and pray that you would too...

This morning, I am reading again the book of Revelation. For years, I have shied away from this particular book because it has made me feel so inept. The interpretations of others over the years have been a little conflicting and puzzling, but on the other end of the spectrum, this book is fearsome! It is the final chapter to the mystery of life! The importance of having some semblance of understanding is paramount for a believer. As I read the very short chapter 10, there is a moment of clarity between life now and life after. The day is coming when the mystery, the bitter sorrows of today will surely pass away. It shall culminate into the sweet and joyful fulfillment of the coming of our Lord and Savior, Jesus Christ! This life may be bitter and sweet, but whosoever shall eat, will "Come" then wash away the former life with the living waters of a life with Jesus. Someday, the mystery of God will unfold. Behold! He is coming soon! He brings eternal life forever and ever! Desire, accept---"Come." Then be---Whosoever...

Whosoever

God asks, "Are you longing to be?
Does your heart thirst for me?"
Taste the bitter and the sweet
Knowing someday we shall meet.

God said, "Come" in a prayer
I say, "Is that You standing there?"
Now Your words fill the air
"Child, I know life is painfully unfair."

But life here and now is very brief
Fear not, find peace and sweet relief
Though the bitter, hard to bear
Will be washed away if you dare.

Dare to "Come" accept my peace
Then pain and sorrow will surely cease
As the final chapter begins to unfold
The Book of Life your hand shall hold.

A revelation, "Come, come to Me!"
My living waters shall set you free
Child of Mine forever and ever
The mystery of God: Whosoever.

Whosoever? Well it is you!
So what then shall you do?
For I promise to leave you never
You are Mine---My Whosoever...

Write Story

I cannot pinpoint the exact moment in time when God called me to write. It seems that the call, the desire, or compulsion, simply comes supernaturally and there is no preparation or thoughts that are my own. It is solely of Him. Often the end or conclusion of the writing is a surprise to me. There are no demands, just a tender pulling on my mind and heart to express words of a spiritual matter and imploring one to acknowledge the gift of His presence and His outflow from a plain, ordinary human being that happens to be---me. It is indescribable, yet there is no denying that God has a hold of this pencil and my hand moves to the spiritual world as it graces this page and words appear in divine array. Not me! Not me! I have nothing to say. It is the blessing that comes when He announces that He is speaking today. There is nothing to do but wait, write and see. God has been incredibly generous to me! No, I cannot pinpoint the exact moment in time when God called me to write. I just do it when He calls; as I am carried to a higher plane, an unknowable height. Could I have ever imagined this gift that awakens in my soul a glimpse into spiritual insight? Most assuredly, no! Yet here He stands, my beloved Lord, guiding the pencil with His hand at the dawn of His sovereign light. Every morning He comes with words, softly speaks this sweet request, "Child of mine---write…"

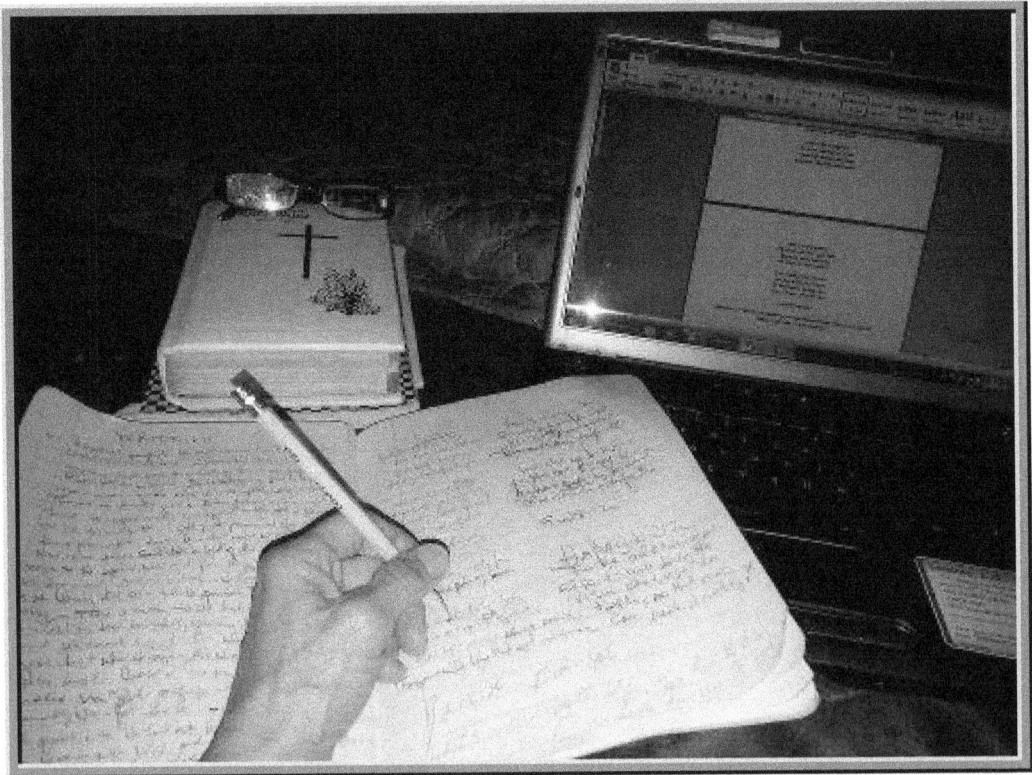

Write

Lord, am I truly ready?
In times such as these
Where fearful hearts cry out
In anguished and fretful pleas.

Lord, could I truly write?
To those suffering in unrest
Could I write, don't fret?
People, it is not your quest!

Lord, write it truly, truly
For those who have no peace
Words will always come, then
Speak love that will never cease!

Lord, it is now written
On weary souls shine Your light
Worry not, oh precious child
His words are surely infinite!

Lord, thank you for this time
And Your words for all to see
My hand guided by Your voice
"Child of mine---write for Me."

❧❧

Then the LORD answered me and said:
"Write the vision
And make it plain on tablets,
That he may run who reads it."

Habakkuk 2:2 (NKJV)

Yes Or No Story

Why do Christians feel so burdened? I can only speak for myself, but there are times that we call, "missed opportunities." We believe that the soul of another, a friend, family member, or even a complete stranger is our sole responsibility in regards to Salvation. We have all heard the teaching for the purpose of our walk. God! Help me, because I am praying the "Yes or No" prayer. I want to place the burden that You and only You bore so horrifically for me; I want to allow You to protect and direct those lost ones waiting to be counted as Yours. I want to surrender the one last remnant of my fear and failure to You. For You cannot fail! The words were on my lips, yet I failed to speak them. The prayer was swirling in my head, yet I failed to pray it. The moment in question weighed me down as I turned back for a final look---I saw love---love was celestially hovering about in the very place where I sat, but thankfully, my God filled the space. My human vocabulary recognized His reassuring comment. "I got this one," He said.

Dear friends, I believe the failure of Christians to impress on others the Divinity of Christ is not unusual, in fact, I think this happens often in our walk. I have felt the burden of walking away in defeat and the weight of being a cowardly Christian was tenderly lifted when He said, "I got this one." And I believe He does, because I sure don't! I do not have it, even though He gave it! Eternity is His to give---When He gave it to me, my life was mine to live. So I have my life with the knowledge that He has made me His. I am His! I never once said, "I got it," but in an instant I knew He gave it. Christians, do not worry about how to save sinners. Whatever words you say or do not say, remember this: Jesus gave it and Jesus will save it! Sometimes I pray and read His extraordinary Word and I wish that God would say these two words---"Yes or No." For those who are so broken and cannot comprehend or simply have not the years, days, hours, or minutes to analyze, sometimes I pray just these two words; "Yes or No." Lord, let it be this simple. If you say "Yes" to God, He will say, "I got this one." Say "No" to God and He will say, "Go then." This is what I know; God will always have it, because He's got it! The question is, do you want Him? If so---ask yourself, "Have I said, "Yes or No?" Is it so simple that one word will decide where I will go?

He says again, "I got this one," then He sits in my vacated place. A tear dries on a pain wracked face; alone, yet not. One word cries--acquiesces, then sighs at last—"Yes."

Yes Or No

Is it yes, or is it no?
Where then Lord shall I go?
In the chair I quietly sit, undone
You say to me, "I got this one."

Oh thank you Father God, I pray
These are my thoughts on this day
For I have failed so miserably
Take this burden of life from me.

Is it yes, or is it no?
Lord, be it simple, be it so
That one would cry to You and say
"God please take this agony away."

A tear dries on a pain wracked face
But He has come to take my place
One word to Him, then acquiesce
Peace comes in the sigh of---"Yes."

Yours Story

I believe there are times when I minimize what God wants to do for me. It is not a lack of faith, but more a lack of confidence that God would pick my mind to run around in. So maybe it sounds odd the way I phrased that, but He seems to flit in and out of my intellect on a daily basis. It always depends on me, and if I make the time to listen to Him. Sometimes I am a little narrow-minded and often surprised at the length He will go through to make a deposit of truth into my intellect. What a patient God He is!

Yours

In that narrow channel of my intellect I cry out to God to widen my mind and pour down wisdom and knowledge, strength and courage to expound and comprehend.

In that narrow channel of my intellect I cry out to God to give to me every fruit that is mine because He has prepared the way for me to accept the gifts.

In that narrow channel of my intellect I cry out to God to broaden the path and carry me in absolute peace to Him and to the path for which I am destined.

In the narrow channel of my intellect I cry out to God to feel the Holy Spirit flood the tiny gate that opens up unto that unfathomable place of joy!

In that narrow channel of my intellect I cry out to God as my heart soars, the words explode onto the paper---not me, not mine, but---Yours…

Absolute Peace Story

These words have embalmed my mind: "Absolute Peace." I thought of those times when I was absolutely in that perfect place. Every moment that played in my heart revealed a warm embrace, or simply words of love. I felt absolute peace when my son told me, "I love you Mom," over the phone. I felt absolute peace when my husband hugged me at my kitchen sink. I felt absolute peace when my best friend kissed me as she was wheeled away to surgery. I felt absolute peace when I found tiny beads in my desk drawer. It was my brother's identification bracelet placed on his ankle over fifty years ago. The day that he was born, I felt absolute peace. I remember making those bracelets when I worked as a nurse in the nursery. I felt absolute peace when I held my very first newborn to my heart. I feel absolute peace when my grandchildren fall onto my lap.

It seems like it was just yesterday when we sat outside and enjoyed dinner with a long-time friend. She wrapped her arms around me and pulled me to her. I felt absolute peace. When someone snapped the picture, I felt it once again. How fantastically real it was to see her face and mine in that moment of absolute peace. When my daughter laughingly assures me that she will never put me in a nursing home, I feel absolute peace.

I feel absolute peace, because someday, I will have absolute peace that is not momentary or fleeting. I feel absolute peace knowing that my God is absolutely real. For it is not about your age, your work, your appearance, or your material belongings. It is an unguarded moment in time when you simply acquiesce, giving in to inexplicable joy. Is it momentary and fleeting? Yes, but it fills you with a desire for life; a desire that makes you run to the elusiveness of, "Absolute Peace."

❧❧

You will keep him in perfect peace,
Whose mind is stayed on You,
Because he trusts in You.
Isaiah 26:3 (NKJV)

Photo Credit: Kent Viklund

Absolute Peace

Something we all search for
It skirts through the mind
A momentary blessing comes
If only we could find.

A perfect place inside us
Where absolute peace prevails
Needing this so badly
When all else fails.

There is only one conclusion
Having given it much thought
Absolute peace is fleeting
Even though earnestly sought.

I've felt it in my lifetime
Memories anchored to my soul
Then shattered into pieces
What was once vibrant, whole.

Absolute peace, an illusion
No, I believe it is real
Thank God for these moments
That allow a body to feel.

How could we survive life
My heart cannot conceive
Warmth touching everywhere
Demands that I believe.

What God alone possesses
So incredibly designed
Absolute peace forevermore
When I leave this world behind.

I am running to absolute peace
Momentary, fleeting, elusive, true
Then I fall into His arms
Shedding every sorrow I ever knew...

The Woman And The Fly Story

What a marvelous time I had that night. I enjoyed an engaging conversation with Crystal Lordi when I introduced her to the amazing Mary Howitt, and her whimsical poem, *The Spider and the Fly*. Some years ago my heart was so touched by the gentleness of Wendy Goldberg when I read her posting on Facebook:

There's a silly old house fly, wandering around my room tonight, and I just can't kill it! I think it's a little slow, maybe old, and I think it's a lady. Round and round my laptop screen, laptop lid, the TV, the phone, my wrist watch...me! I knock "her" out of the way, and she slowly lands somewhere else; doesn't even buzz. I think I'll catch her and let her go outside before I sleep so she won't land on my face.

Here is a lesson in life that is simplistically written. She has a heart so gentle, kind, and loving; with a heart that cannot even kill a fly. She is more than beautiful, and smarter than me. She is the perfect example of the gentle spirit that I have prayed for. Once again I am in awe of my friend of over 40 years.

The Woman And The Fly

God give me patience
Especially as I grow old
Sometimes moving slowly
My actions no longer bold.

Oh, I can barely fly
Looking for a friend
Seeing the light, warmth
If only I could mend.

I used to buzz, I think
Now I no longer make a sound
Landing here, landing there
Seems I just fly round and round.

A gentle voice speaks to me
I know I am being a pest
She swats at me half-heartedly
I am desperately needing a rest.

I am a tired old woman
Then I look into her eyes
Compassion comes to greet me
And I have come to realize.

She will never hurt me
Might move me to another place
Of course she is so beautiful
I might land on her face.

I inhale the fresh crisp air
Even though I cannot see
I will sleep and dream of her
My friend who set me free.

❧

This poem can take you anywhere.

I hope it takes you to patience,

gentleness, acceptance, and love of

all things that God has created...

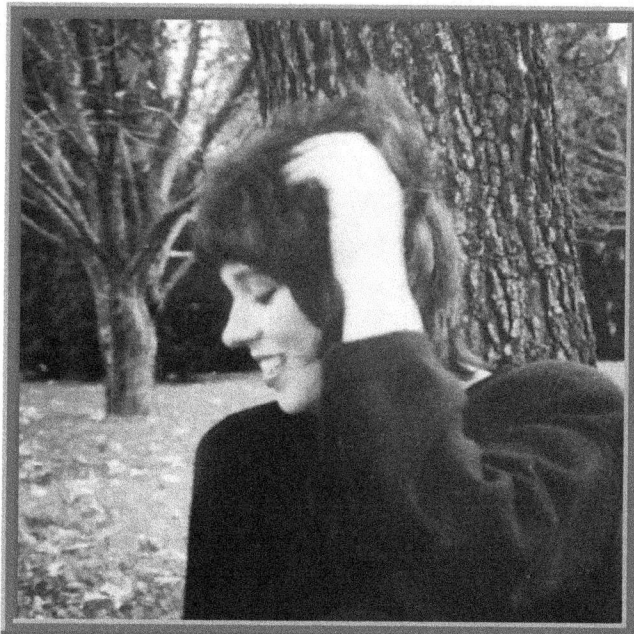

Wendy's Story

When I think of Wendy Goldberg, joy bursts into my heart. I wrote her story some years ago, but I did not finish it right away. Now I know why. After spending precious time over dinner with Wendy and her husband, not that long ago, she remains completely captivating. She has danced in and out of my life for over 40 years. I have never been far from Wendy. Words have not been forthcoming to write because she is almost beyond description. There is absolutely no malevolence in her. We never had one hurtful word between us in all these years. Not one. I give the credit solely to her. She was always very beautiful. She would argue about that as she got older, but she is still beautiful. Wendy has a God given gift that is so rare: unconditional love. I have never met anyone who possesses the ability to love so simplistically and completely.

There was another blessing for me from that night as I observed this same unique gift in her daughter Heidi. And even her dog Quincy, shows unconditional love. I wanted to talk about the precious memories that we have shared over the years.

We danced. How we danced! My life was forever changed because I simply forgot that it was not all filled with sorrow when we were together. Her laughter permeates my being now and always.

I have many delightful memories from our younger years. We had these amazing escapades with our children and adventures that not only we cherish, but even after all these years, our now adult children delight in hearing the stories again and reminiscing about those wonderful times.

I feel young when I am with my dear friend and it seems as if time never changed the gentle heart that remains constant and forever in her and continues to bring joy and laughter when we gather to share a meal and fellowship together. I have begged more than a few meals off my friend as she enjoyed cooking and entertaining in the warmth of her home. If throughout one's lifetime a person would manage to acquire a friend like Wendy, then you have been as blessed as I have been.

Wendy is an artist, and I have taken the liberty to request her permission to use her paintings of her shoes that inspired me to paint poetically with words, of my love for her. I might call them her dancing shoes.

I planed to dance my way to heaven with my friend. I promised to write a song someday of a girl in her dancing shoes. Sadly, that day to write a poem of tribute came sooner than I expected, or would have predicted. As my friend, I had hoped that we would have many more years together, but it was not to be. I thank God for the blessing that she was to me!

Dancing in and out of my life, but she never danced away from me...

Wendy

She brings to me a melody
A song that would surely last
Like a rare and precious gem
She came waltzing into my past.

Remembering every moment
I lost count of all my sighs
Dancing in and out of my life
Tears poured from my eyes.

I promise to write the song
If our story should ever end
As we dance our way to Heaven
I will sing to my precious friend.

Get out those dancing shoes
Then paint a picture for me
Dancing in and out of my life
My friend you will always be.

Friends pass through our lives
The memories flood my mind
One tucked away inside my heart
This treasure my God designed.

Laughter suddenly fills the air
Her dazzling smile I see
Dancing in and out of my life
She never danced away from me.

Oh the years might press on
Hearing a phrase she has said
The purity of her heart revealed
Plays a song inside my head.

I would gladly write the song
Of my captivating friend
Dancing in and out of my life
To a song without an end.

Paintings by Wendy Goldberg ©

131

Forever My Friend

For my precious friend, Wendy Goldberg, who left this world too soon.
This is a song I promised to write for her.

◈

A Time To Dance

Come dance with me,
Forevermore
Hold my hand dear friend
Walk through the door.

Dance away, but wait for me
Dance away still memories stay
Oh, I can see you there
Dancing merrily without a care.

Come dance with me,
Forevermore
Hug me close dear friend
Till our hearts soar.

Come dance with me again
Dance where time will never end
The heavens open wide as music plays
Forevermore, forevermore, my friend…

I love you

My Jim, Sitting Beside Me

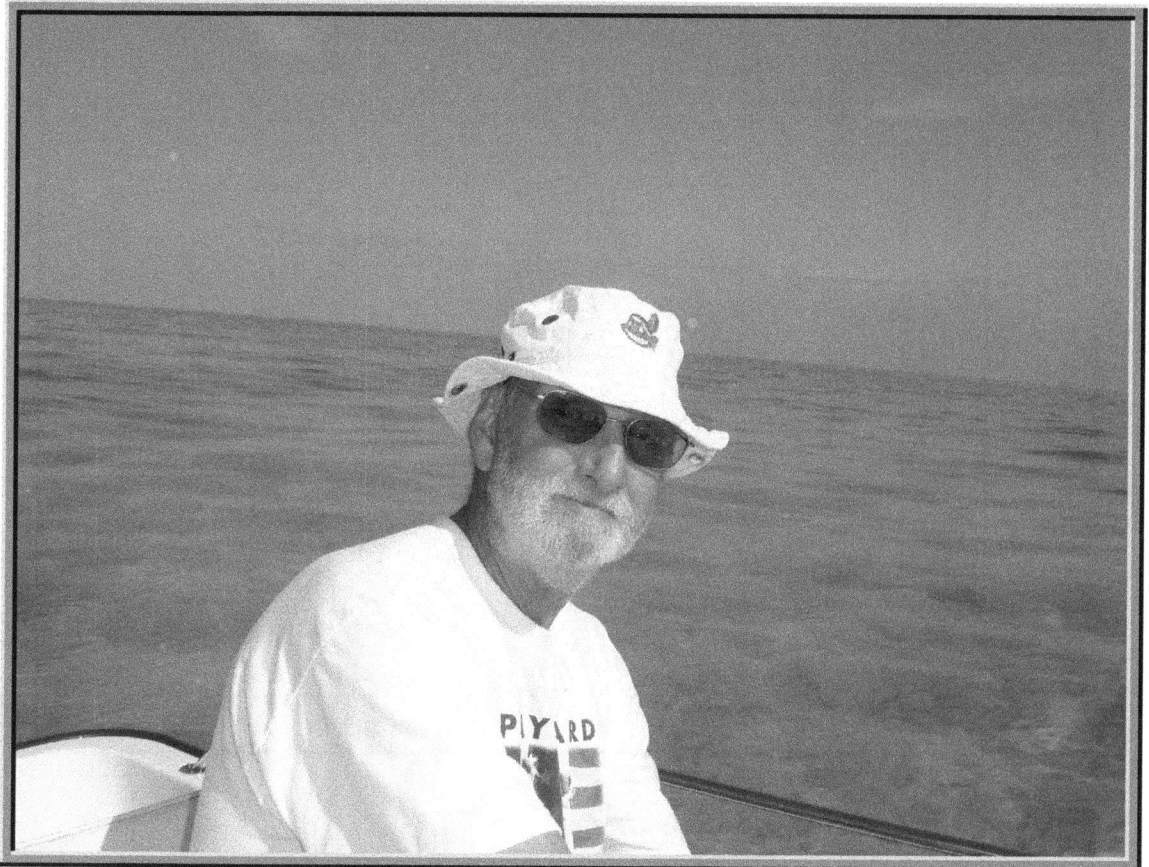

I miss the sun and her warmth
The azure blue waters of the sea
But most of all I miss him
My Jim, sitting beside me.

He was the Captain of the boat
We were destined to be there
I loved the sight and smell of life
As I breathed the salty air.

Through depths unknown beneath us
A vast horizon endless and free
We were on a peaceful journey
Till the sun dipped into the sea.

One day I pray to return to this place
Where it was plain for all to see
Remembering the promise of eternal life
With my Jim sitting beside me…

About The Author

By: Diane Zawilinsky

They say a picture is worth a thousand words. In this book, you will find an artist at work using words to paint pictures with unmatched beauty. As you journey through the writings of Kathleen Higham in this book, you will find these paintings unique in their own way. Unlike paintings you may see displayed on walls in an art gallery, these paintings are displayed on hearts, and open now, for all to see. These paintings from Kathleen portray something much different than a painting on a wall. Some of these paintings portray comfort and peace. Others portray strength and courage. Some portray love and hope while others portray grace and truth. But each and every one portray the glory of God. You will find these paintings have actually been created by the Master's hand. As you read, I pray you find Kathleen's hidden treasures. Her prayer is that you will be comforted by the God of all comfort and that you will experience the peace that passes all understanding. She prays that you come to understand the Source of strength and courage. She prays that you will experience the Love that never fails and that you hold onto the hope of glory. Her prayer is that you will find that His grace is sufficient and that you will find in these painting the truth that will set you free.

For God, who said, "Light shall shine out of darkness," is the One who has shone in our hearts to give the Light of the knowledge of the glory of God in the face of Christ.

2 Corinthians 4:6 (NASB)

Diane Zawilinsky

*Diane and her husband, Pastor Steve Zawilinsky, have served side by side for over 20 years at **Upper Room Ministries** in Austintown, Ohio. She teaches Bible study to the children and teens and counsels along with her husband. They have a weekly Bible ministry at the **Phoenix House** for those who are in need.*

A Note From The Author

Darkness tried to press me down

With unspeakable sorrow and grief

Knowing not that I would turn

To The Comforter for His relief

What was meant for sorrow

Drew me closer to Him instead

Joy came to me so bright

God reached down to hold me

Then surrounded me with His light

For with Him I walk daily

I walk by faith, not by sight.*

This book is titled, **Praise to God,** and it is so very personal to me because it brought forth birth pangs of the deepest sorrow, but my sorrow was thrust upwards to the heavens in utmost joy as I praise my God! I praise my Lord and Savior for His mercy and grace, that once again, carries me to this familiar place. For most assuredly, my life was changed in unimaginable ways, still, I shall praise Him for all of my days. Sorrow and Joy unite with words of love, so that I might see…

PRAISE TO GOD---For He gives yet one more book to me!

In Christ,

Kathleen Higham

෴

* *(For we walk by faith, not by sight:)* 2 Corinthians 5:7 (KJV)

You may contact the author at:

kathleenhigham@yahoo.com

www.wordsoflifepublishing.com

Special thanks to my team:

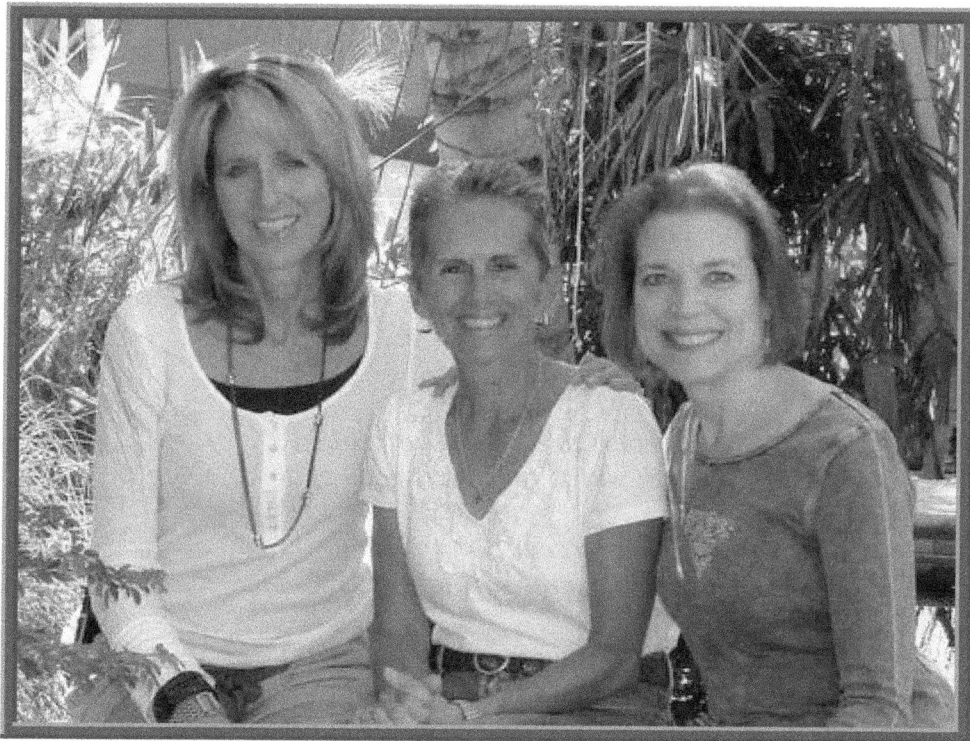

Photo Credit: Patty Polston
Pictured above from left to right: artist Kathleen Denis,
author Kathleen Higham and editor Gloria Dingeldein.

The following pages are an introduction for
my next book which will be titled
God is Love

February Fourteen

February 14, 2015---A Valentine Story Called "End Of Story"

Today on this day for lovers, I ask a question because I am not who I was when I was Jim's wife. And I am surely not the person I was before I met the love of my life! So, show me who I am now, Lord. The mother, the friend, the writer, the...? Well, maybe the questions should be, "What I am going to do with the rest of my life if God continues to gift me with, 'Time?' What shall I do with the time in question?" I question what to do with who I am. "What I will do, and where I will go?"

Of course, I have this 5 star reservation at some future date which has been blocked in, so to speak. But the waiting time is not to be frivolously wasted on all this wondering. Who, what, where, and then the "Why" creeps in, once again. Why do I wonder? Time fritters away as my thoughts cloud the purpose. And I am not speaking of "the cloud" of technology that wants to store my data, no it is the cloud that mystifies and muddies the plan. The plan? Yes, God still has a plan and a purpose for my life. (Jeremiah 29:11). My life did not end when God took Jim to his glory. My plan remains the same: serve God, trust God, and wait on God. Someday, my reservation will welcome me to my heavenly home. Until then, I pray to pursue God's plan to bring Him glory. End of story...

End Of Story

Writers are always enthralled
To that which they have been called.

Yet it seems to tarry some
When off the course God says, "Come."

What! We cry in shocking pain
Was this life lived in vain?

He gives and gives and takes away
There are no words left to say.

When at last numbness wears off
We mutter and complain and scoff.

"Was this not really mine," I cried
God said, "No, it was mine," He sighed.

Fair enough, I am a fool, still
Yet ever faithful, He comes to fill.

Time and living changes all things
Only the Father knows what love brings.

Through my heart a crack is drawn
God says, "Live for Me, life goes on."

No valentine, no candy, no card, no kiss
But only one of these things I miss!

Life, life as it was, forever gone
Still, here I am to meet the dawn.

Live for Christ until that day
Then wait for Him, come what may.

Oh I shall, be called unto His Glory
Fly away to the heavens, End of story.

Life Is An Amazing Journey Story

I don't remember the beginning of my journey, but time has moved me quickly to this very morning. There is so much I would have changed, I think. There is so much I would have done, I think. There is so much I would have said, I think. There is so much I would have learned, I think. If only I had known how fast the journey was going to be. You see dear ones, I was completely unaware of the journey, until one day I called my precious Mom, and unbeknownst to me, she had completed her journey. The impact came much later when the paralyzing sorrow and grief lessened and I was able to comprehend the value of time. "Journey Time." Thankfully, as a daughter, I choose to share my mother's journey, not knowing that someday she would be swept off the path we walked together. I miss our talks; our special times that she made me laugh and cry at the same time. I just miss her, period.

You might wonder about my Dad; well I was completely devastated when my Dad's journey ended so tragically some years ago, but I still had her. My mind, even then, did not comprehend that someday, Mom would also complete the journey. So here

I am probably much closer to the completion than I realize, yet fear is not a factor anymore. But, sorrow and profound loss often breaches my thoughts and pushes its way onto the paper. My journey has not been smooth by any means, and there are no complaints, because I have seen the journey of others who have given me pause to stop dreaming for this life and start praising for the life to come.

Here is the lesson: I cannot make one soul journey with me. I am alone with the One who started all this journey business in the first place. I came into this world with a gush and immediately, she was there. From that moment, until the day she slid silently and slowly to the floor and life was no more, I had journeyed with her. I learned on that day how quickly the journey will end for some and how slowly, for others. But for me, there was no warning. I did not get to say good-bye or tell her how much I loved her. So why am I sharing? Because some of you have absolutely no clue that time is slipping away. If you have a Mom, Dad, sister, brother, grandparent, or even one you once called, "friend," I am telling you flat out, life will end! The journey will end!

If you wake up tomorrow, and someone you once loved has gone to heaven, then it is too late to reach out. You journey on, and they journey not. Is there anyone in your life that matters, or once mattered? I can speak from experience when I say that I have cried myself to sleep asking the question, "Why didn't I just pick up the phone and step back into the journey of that person I loved for so many years and for reasons that do not matter, I allowed myself to walk the other way?" I am going to share the single most heartbreaking moment in my life, and let me clarify that it was not finding my mother's dead body in her home, because I walked the journey with her until that day when she slipped away. She always knew how much I loved her.

My sorrow was riding in the car with a small heavy box on my lap. My brother's ashes seemed light, but heavy. I could not hug him, or tell him I loved him. I could not say these words, "I am sorry that I failed you." Some might say that he failed me, but I know that it was me who stepped off the path of our journey together. His journey ended, and mine continued on. His death was not in vain, because I am willing to stand before you on the path of your journey and ask you, even though you know you have the right of way, please stay. For I am here to tell you that one day it won't matter and that one person who loved you only less than God Himself---yes that one person will come to the end of the journey.

My prayer is that no one would ever feel the weighty sorrow of the one who moved on, because you thought you had the right of way. I speak now! Alter your course before you find yourself alone in deep remorse; talking to yourself about who was wrong or right. It doesn't matter at the journey's end. Your tears will fall upon the empty path where once walked your friend.

I plead with you. Alter your course…

Life Is An Amazing Journey

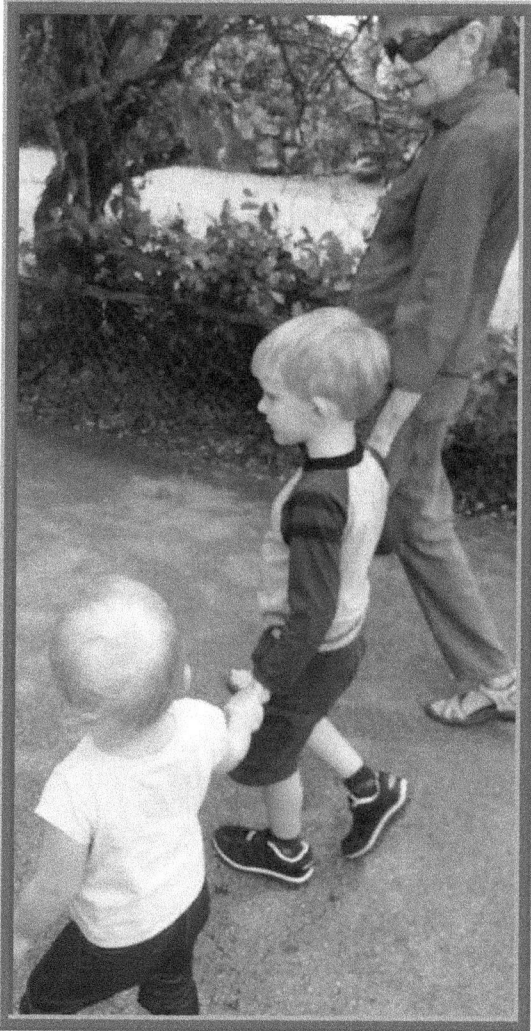

Photo Credit: Kent Viklund

The closer I get in my journey
The slower seems my walk
But my spirit runs in earnest
Even if my heart should balk.

Moving toward the moment
Where time has paved the way
As memories push me onward
To this most inevitable day.

The closer I get in my journey
The less I need to speak
For words once meaningful
Left behind for others to seek.

Moving toward the moment
For what mattered, now does not
Now time has spun the dial
No victory for battles fought.

The closer I get in my journey
On my knees I may crawl
But listening, always listening
To hear the Father's call.

Moving toward the moment
Feel the touch of my Friend
He picks me up and carries me
To the place of my journey's end.

❧❦

Life is an amazing journey. The beginning is fast and furious.
The middle may be meticulous and curious, but the end, slow and serious.
Life is an amazing journey. But, the most amazing journey of all is the one that
lacks remorse; a journey of love and forgiveness for the one who altered the course.
Life is an amazing journey…

141

Taco's Story

I held my very sick dog, Taco Bella, close to my heart. It was September 1, 2015. She was not trembling, but trusting me for her care. Taco's Veterinarian, Dr. Cheryl Whitfield, explained to me that Taco would feel no pain and simply drift away. So I was led to a soft chair with Taco cradled in my arms, wrapped in her old familiar blanket. She looked at me with brown eyes that said, "It's Ok." Dr. Cheryl and Dana, Taco's favorite persons at Austintown Veterinary Clinic, sat down on the floor in front of me and we prayed together. I asked God to give me strength to end her suffering as I nodded my head "Yes" to the doctor, and in a moment, Taco went to heaven. I wish to take this time to thank Dr. Whitfield and Dana and all of the staff who work for Austintown Veterinary Clinic for their excellence and compassionate care for God's creatures. It was an intimately sad time that I shared with these two women, and yet, there was no rush. I held my precious dog to my heart for a long time after she died, and these dear women stayed with me. It has been a long two years since Jim went to heaven on September 16, 2013. I felt a warmth come over me, and it was a letting go feeling as her tiny body molded to mine, and it brought me peace. Her grieving for Jim was over. As she lay against my breast, there was a calming rest. She went to heaven on that morning to be with her best friend and mine. I cried so many tears, but it seemed to be a completeness and washing away of sorrow. I told my friend, Diane, about the peace I felt in those last minutes that I held Taco and this is what she expressed to me: "In that moment in time you held Taco to your heart, Jim was holding her too. "You were together, the three of you, and God allowed you to feel the peace of the grand reunion that waits for you someday." I was stunned by this magnificent thought. Praise God for His unfailing love and mercy.

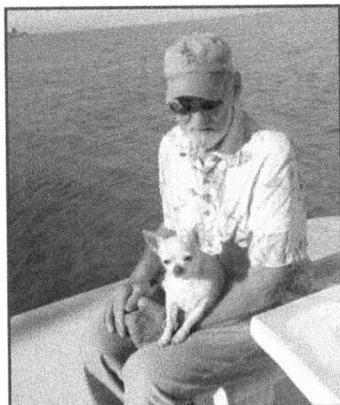

I breached the heavenly realm
And felt my Father's sigh
"Feel my peace, oh child of mine,
For you shall never die."

My loved ones wait in joyful hope
As their peace floods my heart
For me, my Jim and Taco
Are only briefly apart.

Praise to God, precious ones
Someday He will come for me
Then together with our Father God
Together, forever we will be.

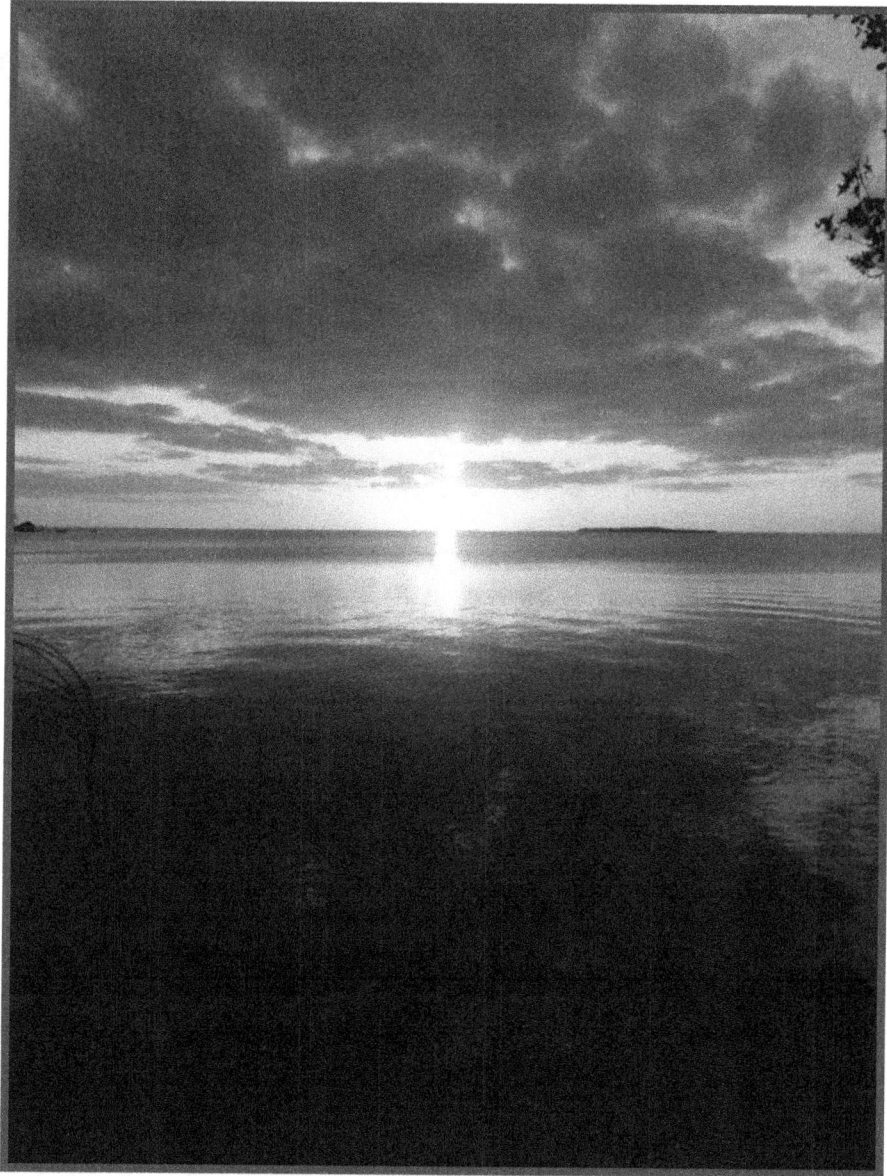

From the rising of the sun to its going down
The LORD's name is to be praised.

Psalm 113:3 (NKJV)

Oh, give **thanks** *to the* LORD,

for He is **good!**

for His **mercy**

endures

forever.

Psalm 118:1 (NKJV)

Kathleen Higham

Author Kathleen Higham, shown here on a beautiful Spring day enjoying Mill Creek Park. She enjoys meeting and interacting with people around the world, as God opens doors for her to share her gift of poetry and praise to God, to comfort and encourage others in their walk of life.

By Him therefore
let us offer the Sacrifice of
Praise to God
continually,

Hebrews 13:15a

Kathleen Higham listens intently to God, and then she faithfully writes it down by hand. She is a true writer and poet that ministers to the soul, using everyday experiences and situations as her canvas, she interweaves descriptions of fierce storms, magnificent humming birds, gorgeous flowers, fantastic friendships, the beauty of life and the hope of everlasting life after death. She paints pictures with well chosen words that clearly reveal the love our Savior Jesus Christ has so dearly bestowed upon mankind. May you be richly blessed.

Brenda D. Sereday

$10.00
ISBN 978-0-9896973-1-6
51000>

9 780989 697316